Japanese Film History

Preface

To many, Japan is both familiar and mysterious. Whenever Japan is mentioned, people are reminded of cherry blossoms, samurai, and Mt. Fuji, whereas words such as modesty, politeness and precision are often used to describe Japanese people. Japan, well known for its cultural label of "The Chrysanthemum and The Sword", cannot rid itself of its innate contradictory character. This most westernized East Asian nation often gives out the typical eastern conservative impression; its people widely known as "modest and humble" frequently reveal their insolent and tyrannical nature.

The world knows Japanese films, but how well? Akira Kurosawa (黒澤明) and Yasujiro Otsu (小津安二郎) have long held a place among the gods of cinema and been put on a pedestal. From the day Rashomon (羅生門) won in the Venice Film Festival to the increasingly higher ranking of the more recent Tokyo Story (東京物語) on Greatest Films in History, the world has seen increasing appreciation and admiration towards Japanese films.

However, most people's understanding towards Japanese films does not go beyond that. A misunderstanding exists where it is believed only a handful of famous directors' names could represent Japanese cinema, yet it certainly is not that simple, as Japan's film history has spanned over 100 years. Since film's s introduction into Japan in the late 19th century, Japanese film has deeply been branded with its own culture. For a long period of time, like historical Japan itself, Japan's film industry was an isolated island. All processes from production, management, to review and release evolved and grew on their own, independent from other countries, misleading people into thinking a few directors represented the whole of Japanese films. This self-contained system also makes it difficult for people from the outside to truly gain a holistic view of what goes on inside. Therefore, to the whole wide world of film audiences, Japanese cinema, like its mysterious nation itself, is veiled with a layer of mystery.

This book aims to lead readers closer into the world of Japanese cinema and its history over the last 100 years. Though it is difficult to provide a detailed and accurate account, this book covers the majority and most important elements. The author hopes more readers interested in Japanese cinema will gain a better understanding toward Japanese films and a better insight into the culture behind them.

Chapter 1 Silent Films 1896-1931

1 Introduction of Films

Only one year after the Lumiere brothers screened their first film, "Arrival of a Train at a Station", at a Paris cafe, this new thing "film" was brought into Japan. The projection device at the time was called a cinematograph, and the films were simply groups of photographs.

It was not until 1898 that Japanese people truly saw their very first film: one shot in Japan by the Lumiere brothers to portray Japanese customs and traditions. In the same year, Asano Shiro (浅野四郎), a cinematographer at Konishi Photography Company, made Japan's very own first film.

It is worth mentioning here that from its birth, Japanese cinema has formed indissoluble ties with Japanese traditional theater. Early Japanese films mostly covered kabuki (歌舞伎) and bunraku (文楽) content; their filming techniques and methods of expression were largely borrowed from traditional theater and visual arts. Using this new and fresh technology to tell the tales people were familiar with, Japanese films created the sense of recognition and familiarity in Japanese people and were readily accepted as a new form of entertainment. Since then, seeking inspiration and source material from traditional theater has become a custom of Japanese film.

2. Earliest director- Shozo Makino マキノ省三

Japan's early films, similar to the ones around the world, were often simple recordings of people and objects. As long as true elements in life could be transported onto negatives, it could be called a film. A narrative story would merely be the "director" filming the performance process. There was, for quite a long period after filming was born, no real directing.

Just as Georges Méliès is to France, and Griffith to America, Japan naturally had its first director: Shozo Makino (マキノ省三).

Before Shozo Makino (1878-1929) came into contact with films, he had been a Bunraku performer and theater owner. Naturally, the source of his films often came from Bunraku. He directed, not from a script, but from memory, guiding the actors based on the plots and lines from countless Bunraku plays he had learned by heart.

Makino's milestone work was Chushingura (忠臣蔵) filmed in 1910. This 80-minute-long film was completed using panoramic images with each shoot lasting 1 to 2 minutes. Chushingura is a well-known samurai revenge story in Japan and used to be frequently performed in both Kabuki and Bunraku forms. Makino was the first one to express the story in film format and created in his version many essential elements later considered indispensable in a film.

Since the filming of Chushingura, this story has been remade repeatedly. It has been said that there are more than 80 editions of the film. Some even joked that if one wants to know all the Japanese film stars, he or she only needs to look them up in all editions of Chushingura. Though a casual remark, it is not too far from the truth: many film stars of different periods have had lead roles in Chushingura.

Another important fact that deserves to be mentioned here is the lead actor Matsunosuke Onoe (尾上松之助). He followed and worked with Makino on many films and quickly became the first film star in Japanese film history. His cooperation with Makino was also considered the first star director and actor collaboration in Japan.

3. Japanese Silent Film's Specialty- Benshi （弁士）

In Japan's Silent Film period, one feature that distinguishes itself from the rest of the world and must be mentioned here is the existence of "benshi".

Silent films were of course soundless. In most cinemas around the world, major plots had to be shown in title cards, and the only voice audiences could hear was that of a piano, played live in the theater.

However, Japanese audiences could hear another voice, the voice of a benshi. Benshi was Japan's professional film narrator. This profession emerged from audiences' need to understand the complications of plots in films, which could be hard to understand with only the help of a few title cards; moreover, Japanese audiences were not used to reading title cards and benshis were able to narrate for them and help them comb through plots. As benshis became more and more common, their value rose and their roles went further than narration, with benshis even adding their own commentaries and interpretations. They even adjusted the speed of the film at will, based on their preferences and their narration need. For the same reason, the same silent film, when narrated by different benshis, could generate completely different experience. Some glib and quick-tonged benshis could become the biggest stars in the film industry. Japanese audiences at the time would not choose films to watch based on directors and actors, but benshis. An outstanding benshi could lead audiences along the plot development of the film while a terrible benshi could possibly dismantle a film into broken pieces.

As the profession of the benshi further matured and developed, the requirement and management of benshis became more formalized in the film industry. Later benshis had to hold certifications in order to be employed. The existence of benshis made it easy for Japanese audiences to transition smoothly from a dramatic stage performance to a silent world. However, benshis also sustained Japanese audiences' resistance towards sound films, which will be further discussed later on.

4. Appearance of Actresses

Apart from benshis, another area that distinguishes early Japanese films from the rest of the world lies in the non-existence of actresses. Early Japanese films only had male actors, the same as traditional Japanese theater.

Traditionally in Japan, females could not act in theater plays; therefore, early Japanese films followed suit with men playing both female and male roles, similar to how Beijing Opera was traditionally done. However, in American films of this period, the number of female stars was far greater than male stars; America also had a star system where one famous film star could ensure success at the box office. As a large quantity of films produced in Europe and America had entered Japan since the end of World War I, it had a huge impact on Japanese film industry. The star system, in particular, gave Japanese film producers new insight and inspiration.

Therefore, Japan producers started to seek their own female star and Shochiku (松竹) Film Studio was the first to try. They started an actors' training school. After that, more and more actresses exited Shochiku's training and entered the film industry. Shochiku adopted the star system from Hollywood and a film production was often centered on one star. The earliest group of female stars such as Yuriko Hanabusa (英百合子), Kurishima Sumiko (栗島纯子), Michiko Hayama (叶山三千子) all appeared during this time period, with Kurishima Sumiko (栗島すみ子) holding the title of Japan's first great female star.

The emergence of female actors and stars had a profound significance on the history of Japanese cinema People will soon realize that the most influential actors during Japanese films' golden age were almost all female, and several film masters' works were centered on a certain famous female star. This will be further discussed in Chapter 4.

5 Yasujiro Ozu 小津安二郎 & Mikio Naruse's 成瀬巳喜男 Working-Class Drama (庶民劇 shomin-geki)

During silent film period, a few later-famous directors started their film career and were beginning to establish their unique styles people would soon become very familiar with. The top two directors would be Yasujiro Ozu and Mikio Naruse.

Ever since they became famous, these two directors have been frequently mentioned together. They both often made films about the middle class and common people. The biggest similarities between the two actually already existed during early silent film period. The protagonists in their films were often common people making a worldly living. This type of films was often called working-class drama - shomingeki.

Ozu's "shomingekis" were often commended for their visual creativity and sense of humor. His early films' subjects were burlesque and ridiculous farce comedies. Ozu himself watched many European and American movies and his own films revealed traces of influence from Howard Hawks, Ernst Lubitsch, and King Vidor. Ozu filmed many of his productions during the silent film period and unfortunately many of them have not survived. His masterpieces were "I Was Born, But..." (生れてはみたけれど, *Umarete wa mita keredo*) and "A Story of Floating Weeds" (浮草物語, *Ukigusa monogatari*), both of which reflected many of Ozu's own experiences and thoughts. The former film showed many mature filming techniques whereas the latter was remade into a sound film "Floating Weeds" (浮草, *Ukigusa*) in 1959.

Naruse's silent films were similar to Ozu's, to some extent. He gained his fame through sarcastic comedies like "Flunky, Work Hard" (小人物，加油吧, *Koshiben, ganbare*). Though they are naturally different from Ozu's slapstick, the humor and sarcasm certainly could be traced to the same origin. Later on in Naruse's career, he gradually developed his own unique themes and filming style. Several of his social problem dramas like "Apart From You" (君と別れて, *Kimi to wakarete*)" had female protagonists and revealed social criticism and a bleak and pessimistic outlook, which was his well-known style. This unique style was further developed in his early sound films such as "Wife, Be Like a Rose" (妻よ薔薇のやうに, *Tsuma yo bara no yo ni*)" and "Three Sisters with Maiden Hearts" (乙女ごころ三人姉妹, *Otome-gokoro - Sannin-shimai*).

6. Teinosuke Kinugasa's Rise to Fame 衣笠貞之助

Another important director during the silent film period is Teinosuke Kinugasa (1896-1982). He was born into a tobacconist family in Kameyama, Mie Prefecture. In his early years, he was an *oyama* (女形) and played female roles in Kabuki, and from 1917 on, took on similar roles in silent films. Since the introduction of actresses, Kinugasa changed his career and went into directing. He made his directorial debut in 1920. In 1929, he travelled to Europe and Russia to learn western filming techniques. In his whole life, he directed altogether 118 films.

One of his important films is "A Page of Madness" (狂った一頁, *Kurutta Ippēji*). It is about psychopaths in an insane asylum. In the film, he used chiaroscuro photography, rapid crosscutting of images, elaborate costumes, props and sets, quite similar to those of the German expressionists. This film was also considered too avant-garde, as many viewers could not follow the pace of the plots and would only grasp some of the key plots, even with the narration and commentaries from benshis.

Kinugasa next directed "Crossroads" (十字路, *Jujiro*), "An Actor's Revenge"(雪之丞变化, *Yukinojo Henge*), and "The Snake Princess" (蛇姬様, *Hebihime-sama*), all of which were quite highly regarded. He leapt to become the most influential director of the time. His long-term collaborator, actor Hasegawa Kazuo (長谷川一夫) also became more and more popular and later rose to be the biggest actor in Japanese cinema at the time. Interestingly, Hasegawa usually played the role of a gentle and cultivated young man, quite similar to what Kinugasa was like when he himself was an actor.

7. The Influence of Daisuke Ito 伊藤大輔 and Masahiro Makino マキノ雅弘

In Japan's late silent film period, a new genre started to gain popularity and later known to the world as particularly Japanese: period film (時代劇, *Jidaigeki*) . Jidaigeki referred to films that are set in the Edo period of Japanese history, before the 1868 Meiji Restoration. They often depict Japanese historical events and characters, showing the lives of samurais, farmers, craftsman and merchants. An important subcategory of jidaigeki is chambara (チャンバラ), depicting swordsmanship and fights. Chambara is exclusively Japanese and its significance to Japan is equivalent to Westerns in the U.S. or Kungfu films in China. Samurai, Japan's historically unique warrior group, bore with them the core values in Japanese traditional culture – the warrior way (武士道, *bushido*). Therefore, other than the martial fighting scenes, chambara often includes exploration and deliberation of bushido spirit. In some aspects, Japan's samurai class, America's cowboys, and China's rogue kungfu warriors share some resemblances, thus making it natural for America's westerns, Japan's chambara, and China's kungfu films to learn from each other, at the same time, to be influenced by each other.

In Japan's Age of Silent Films, two directors made profound and everlasting contributions to the Jidaiheki genre. They are Daisuke Ito and Masahiro Makino.

Daisuke Ito (1898-1981) is Japan's earliest director recognized for his splendid motion shots. Before him, jidaigekis were usually filmed with a camera fixed at one spot, with actors performing right in front of the camera. However, Daisuke Ito was able to arrange a fighting scene where he would carry the camera to walk around actors to film. This major improvement in set management has been studied and copied by many directors ever since.

Daisuke himself also earned the acclaim of "Father of Japanese Jidaigeki". His "Diary of Chuji's Travels" (忠次旅日記, *Chuji tabi nikki*) remains to be a classic that people relish and take delight in.

Masahiro Makino (1908-1993), son of Shozo Makino, became very familiar with film making, under his father's influence. His portrayal of characters' emotions and feelings was famous and considered outstanding at the time. His subjects often showed a sense of criticism and revolt against authorities. His progressive values earned him praise.

It could be said that Daisuke Ito and Masahiro Makino have had an indelible effect on Japan's jidaigekis' development in two aspects: filming techniques and theme exploration. Their respective works "Diary of Chuji's Travels" and "Singing Lovebirds" (鴛鴦歌合戦, *Oshidori utagassen*) were included in the top 100 films of 20th Century in Japan by Kinema Junpo.

Chapter 2 Early Sound Film Era 1931-1939

1. Decline of Benshis

In 1927, when "Jazz Singer" was released and became a box office hit, cinema entered into the new era of sound films. However, on the far side of the Pacific Ocean, this revolutionary leap for Japan, when compared with western countries, seemed to have taken longer to happen.

In Western countries, when the new element "sound" was introduced into the film industry, substantial changes in film making ensued. Directors, actors and technicians all constantly came up with ways to take the most advantage of the use of sound. However, thanks to benshis, sound was nothing new to Japanese film makers and audiences.

They were used to appreciating films while listening to the narration of benshis; the only difference for them would be hearing the sounds from the film directly instead of from benshis.

When sound films were finally introduced to Japan, many cinemas would intentionally turn down the film volume and continue to have benshis narrate the films. As Japanese had long been used to listening to benshis' narration and commentaries, coupled with the fact that their English language level was generally low, the popularization of sound films encountered much more resistance in Japan than in other countries. Benshis, for their own interest, even formed their own organizations to fight against sound films.

However, with the wave of sound films getting stronger and stronger around the world, Japanese audiences started to notice the various differences and discrepancies between benshi's narrations and the original films' dialogs; at times, their narrations would be obviously off the point. Film companies then started to provide Japanese subtitles for foreign films, which became a custom that is still in use today. Therefore, the era of professional benshis slowly declined in the face of technological innovations.

2. Three Film Studios

By the 1930s, almost all silent films were replaced by sound films. There are three film studios who were the most active and important producers for a long time and must be mentioned here.

Nikkatsu Corporation 日活

Founded in 1912, Nippon Katsudō Shashin kabushiki kaisha (日活株式会社, abbreviated into Nikkatsu Corporation) is the oldest professional film studio. Before then, film studios in Japan were mostly small-scale mal-managed family-based-workshop style businesses. Even Nikkatsu was merged from four companies: Yoshizawa Shōten (吉沢商店), M. Pathe Shokai (M・パテ一商会), Fukuhōdō (福宝堂), and Yokota Shōkai (横田商会) from Kyoto.

Nikkatsu established two production studios in Mukojima and Kyoto respectively.

Mukojima Studio focused on new school drama (新派劇, *Shinpageki*), whereas Kyoto focused on period films (jidaigeki). Since then, Tokyo and Kyoto became the symbol of shinpageki and jidaigeki respectively in the film industry for more than 50 years, which was a unique phenomenon in Japan.

Under the leadership of director Eizo Tanaka(田中栄三), Mukojima Studio intensified its filming on melodramas and hired new directors such as Kensaku Suzuki (鈴木謙作) and Kenji Mizoguchi (溝口健二). Recruiting such new promising and talented directors also became an important character of Nikkatsu for many years. Unfortunately in 1923 Great Kanto earthquake, Mukojima Studio was seriously damaged; as a result, key film crew and actors joined the Kyoto Studio one after another.

Since the addition of Mukojima staff, the Kyoto Studio also started filming more contemporary themes, as shown in "Seisaku's Wife" (清作の妻, *Seisaku no tsuma*) by Minoru Murata (村田實), *A Paper Doll's Whisper of Spring* (紙人形の春の囁き *Kami-Ning-Yo Haru No Sasayaki*) by Kenji Mizoguchi, *Five Women Around Him* (彼を繞る五人の女, *Kare o meguru gonin no onna*) by Yutaka Abe (阿部豊). However, the Studio's focus remained on jidaigekis, such as "The Magic Sword" (丹下左膳, *Tange Sazen*), "The Sword of Doom" *(*大菩薩峠, *Dai-Bosatsu Toge),* "Samurai Miyamoto Musashi" (宮本武蔵).In 1934, Nikkatsu rebuilt its base in Tokyo and Negishi Kanichi (根岸寛一) was recruited from his previous reporter post as the head of Tamagawa Studios. He imported the most advanced recording equipment of the time and specialized in making sound films of contemporary themes. Tomu Uchida (内田吐夢) and Tomotaka Tasaka (田坂具隆) became the main creative force behind Tamagawa and their films attracted a large young audience. In 1941, the Studio was forced to close down due to World War II.

Since the 1960s, due to the increasing popularity of television, film audience numbers drastically decreased. In order to remain profitable, Nikkatsu made a fairly big adjustment in their production policy and made films such as "Season of the Sun" (太陽の季節, *Taiyo no kisetsu*), "Crazed Fruit" (狂った果実, *Kurutta kajitsu*),　"Backlight" (逆光線, *Gyakkosen*), designed for the youth market, which led to Nikkatsu Youth Film's golden age. This period also saw many talented directors such as Shohei Imamura (今村昌平), Kiriro Urayama (浦山桐郎), and Kei Kuma (熊井啓). After 1970s, Nikkatsu encountered financial difficulties, therefore, switch to making low-budget pink films (soft-core pornography), which, to some extent, tarnished its many years of good reputation.

Shochiku 松竹

Shochiku Kabushiki Kaisha (松竹株式会社) (abbreviated into Shochiku) evolved from the original kabuki theater founded by Takejirō Otani (大谷竹次郎) in Kyoto, and got its name from the kanji characters "take" 竹 in Takejirō Otani, combined with "matsu" 松 in Matsujirō Shirai (白井松次郎).

Shochiku created its movie studio in Kamata, Tokyo in 1920 and was accomplished in making fastidious working class dramas (庶民劇, shomin-geki), historically known as "Kamata Style". After 1920's Great Kanto Earthquake, a branch in Kamata was opened but closed in 1965. In 1934, Kamata Studio was relocated to nearby Ofuna; Shiro Kido became the head of the Studio and created its modern and comedic "Ofuna Style".

Many nationally acclaimed directors such as Yasujiro Ozu (小津安二郎), Keisuke Kinoshita (木下惠介), Hiroshi Shimizu (清水宏), Nagisa Oshima (大島渚), and Masahiro Shinoda (篠田正浩) came through Shochiku. During the 60s, directors like Oshima, Ozu, and Kinoshita initiated the New Wave Cinema Movement right at Shochiku. With these revolutionary and rebelling young filmmakers changing and uplifting the face of Japan's film industry, Shochiku was considered as the trendsetter.

Apart from film, Shochiku also launched business in theater performances right from the start, ranging from Kabuki, nogaku (能楽, Japanese opera), hi-hi (Japanese comedy duo: manzai kombi 漫才) to symphony orchestra. The well-known Kabukiza in Tokyo and Shijyo Minamiza in Kyoto were theaters both created and owned by Shochiku.

Shochiku also worked with other film studios to be involved in founding Fuji TV Station. It also has created several satellite TV channels that show its own or rebroadcast films and TV series.

Toho 東宝

Tōhō Kabushiki-kaisha Toho Co. Ltd (東宝株式会社, abbreviated into Toho) was founded in 1932 as the Tokyo-Takarazuka Theater Company.

Toho started as a theater company and expanded into the film industry later on. It was originally the Sound Film PCL (写真化学研究所, Photo Chemical Laboratory) established in 1930. This PCL decided to make its own films in 1933, so it recruited its film crew and the widely known Akira Kurosawa joined in at this time.

PCL adopted modern management guidelines from the very beginning and set up the earliest producer system in Japan, making it the most Westernized Japanese film studio. As a result, there appeared the earliest group of avant-garde and leftist film makers. Whether surrealists, or socially critical leftists, all could show their talent in filmmaking at PCL.

PCL went through many difficulties in the beginning. Due to lack of its own distribution route, its films were not easily distributed. In 1937, after merging with the theater company *Takarazuka Kagekidan* (宝塚歌劇団), managed by the railroad magnate Ichizo Kobayashi (小林一三), PCL officially changed its name to Toho. Backed by Kobayashi's substantial financial resources, Toho solved its distribution problem and even put in more investment to recruit talented and promising filmmakers. One after another, a few directors and actors who have already obtained good reputation joined Toho.

Akira Kurosawa (黒澤明) was the director that gained most fame for Toho. Before the 70s, he had been a filmmaker at Toho and many of his films were classics and drew large audiences. Another major director at Toho is Mikio Naruse (成瀬巳喜男). Chapter 4 will cover the experiences and accomplishments of these two directors in detail.

Other than becoming a huge commercial success and fostering many exceptional directors, another area about Toho that is worth praising lies in its championing Japan's social morality. To this day, Toho has never made one film that goes against social ethics and has always been praised by audiences.

Apart from film related industries, quite a few well-known theaters including Japan's first western theater – Imperial Garden theater (帝国劇場, *Teikoku Gekijō*) - in Tokyo are owned by Toho. Toho was also one of the initiators for the establishment of 1959 Fuji TV Station.

3. Kenji Mizoguchi's Masterpiece 溝口健二

In the 30s, a young director, a bold innovative spirit with extraordinary creativity, and a knack for spotting the newest trend, caught the attention of Japan's film industry. This grandmaster is world-famous Kenji Mizoguchi.

Born in 1898, Mizoguchi entered the film industry in 1923, initially wanting to be an actor but ending up as a director's assistant. At the end of 1922, there was a huge staffing change within Nikkatsu. With many actors and directors leaving, Mizoguchi was promoted to director.

In 1923, Mizoguchi created one of Japan's earliest expressionist films, "The Resurrection of Love" (愛に甦へる日, *Ai-ni yomigaeru hi*), also his very first film, which was very well received. Mizoguchi's silent films were mainly new school tragedies like: 1923 "Song of Failure" (敗残の唄は悲し, *Haisan no Uta wa Kanashi*), 1926 *A Paper Doll's Whisper of Spring* (紙人形の春の囁き, *Kami-Ning-Yo Haru No Sasayaki*), 1929 *Bridge of Japan* (日本橋, *Nihonbashi*) and 1933 *Cascading White Threads/White Threads of the Waterfall* (滝の白糸, *Taki no Shiraito*). Films made in the late silent film periods were considered his first major achievements.

Being always hardworking and eager to learn, Mizoguchi researched and explored knowledge regarding traditional Japanese theater such as kabuki, nogaku (能楽), bunraku (文楽), and hogaku, traditional Japanese ensemble music; therefore, many traditional theater elements can always be seen in his films. Mizoguchi's love towards traditional theater drew him into traditional folk customs and culture.

Once Mizoguchi entered the sound film era, he consciously presented and expressed these customs and habits, thus creating his famous naturalist realism style. The protagonists in his movies are usually geishas and actors, through whom he is able to demonstrate to audiences in one aspect Japanese traditional cultures and customs, and in another, the struggles and misfortunes this special group had, thus projecting his strong criticism of society. The prevailing unhealthy phenomena such as money worship, human selfishness, hypocrisy and greed, and the severe class difference between different groups of people all became the targets of Mizoguchi's criticism.

Mizoguchi often used heroines who either became innocently sacrificed or bravely contested with their unjust fates in a male dominated society. Though the endings for these women were inevitably tragic, as individual effort under the strong social system often came to nothing, Mizoguchi was able to show audiences these females' strength and nobility. They constantly seek the freedom of love and go after their dream life. On the other hand, Mizoguchi's male roles are usually selfish, weak and unable to take responsibilities. Interestingly, Mizoguchi himself was slightly like his film characters; he was brought up by his sister and spent much time with different geishas and was certainly not very responsible. Maybe his film characters were a display of his dissatisfaction towards himself, showing his self-criticism. The male characters are willing to forsake women for money, power and status; whereas women in Mizoguchi's films are ready to sacrifice themselves for the men they love, as in the most typical example "The Story of the Last Chrysanthemums" (残菊物語, *Zangiku monogatari*).

Several of his great films including "Sisters of the Gion" (祇園の姉妹, *Gion no kyōdai*), "Naniwa Elegy" aka *Osaka Elegy* (浪華悲歌, *Naniwa hika* or *Naniwa erejī*) and "The Story of the Last Chrysanthemums" were all produced from this period and exhibited those said themes and characters, which all established the foundation for Mizoguch's master position in Japanese cinema.

4. Unique Hiroshi Shimizu 清水宏

Other than Yasujiro Ozu, 1930s' Shochiku had another pillar director, the unique Hiroshi Shimizu (1903-1966).

Even early in the silent film period, Shimizu already used avant-garde filming techniques and liked to employ weird picture composition and film editing, which often surprised audiences. The 1930s saw his increasing improvisation and individualization in film making. He disliked filming in studios and on sets, and preferred shooting on location. Shimizu is also one of the earliest directors who used non-professional actors. In his films, there were many amateur actors with no experience, including children. These non-professionals would start acting as professionals after his simple guidance. He believed that shooting on location and using non-professionals made his films more realistic.

Shimizu's films covered a wide range of themes, which could be easily seen in the large quantity (163) of films he directed. Many of his films such as "Four Seasons of Children" (子供の四季, *Kodomo no shiki)* and "Children in the Wind" (風の中の子供, *Kaze no nakano kodomo*) shared a common characteristic named Children's Perspective. If Ozu's low angle shooting presented more human sympathy, Shimizu's children's angle showed the true picture of the natural and human world. Children's angles also allowed Shimizu to add a sense of play throughout his films, which either made plots more comedic or dramatized the characters' performances. Shimizu's use of children's angles and special shots formed the unique charm of his films. He did not intentionally avoid the ugliness of human nature or the life struggles; instead, with a humorous touch, he created a true and moving common world through good intentions, tolerance and kindness

5. Other Key Directors

The 1930s was the first flourishing period in Japan's film industry. Other than Kenji Mizoguchi and Hiroshi Shimizu, there were also many other excellent directors coming into prominence.

Sadao Yamanaka 山中貞雄

Sadao Yamanaka (1909-1938) was known as the "Jean Vigo" of Japan. This came from his similar fine descriptions of reality and vivid portrayal of his characters. It possibly also had something to do with both of them dying young.

Sadao began his career in the film industry in 1927, directed his first film in 1932, and was instantly regarded as a talented young director. Within 5 years, he then churned out 26 period films (jidaigeki). Unfortunately, only three of his films survived World War two: "The Million Ryo Pot" (丹下左膳余話 百萬両の壺, *Tange sazen yowa:hyakuman ryō no tsubo*), "Humanity and Paper Balloons" (人情紙風船, *Ninjokkamifusen*), "Priest of Darkness" (河内山宗俊, *Kōchiyama sōshun*). Just in these three films, Sadao's master filmmaking skills can be easily seen. Through some simple handling of details and dialogs, he was able to completely unfold a character's personality and qualities. His films are not only active and lively, but also encompass his love and passion towards others.

In 1937, on the day his best work "Humanity and Paper Balloons" premiered, he was drafted into the Japanese army to invade China, was never able to return to his homeland, and died in the then-Japanese-ruled Manchukuo, known today as Manchuria.

Hiroshi Inagaki 稲垣浩

Hiroshi Inagaki (1905-1980) was introduced into the film industry in 1922 through his father's friend. He worked as the associate director to Teinosuke Kinugasa (衣笠貞之助) in his early years. He also participated in making Minoru Murata's and Sadao Yamanaka's films. Once he became a director himself, he focused on period films. His jidaigekis differ from the period films that showed samurai's heroism; instead, he tenderly portrayed the lonely wanderers. For this, his films often touched and reached the heart of the common public in Japan.

After the war, he cooperated with Toshiro Mifune (三船敏郎) on many excellent films. In 1955, his "Samurai I: Musashi Miyamoto" (宮本武蔵) won Oscar Academy Award for Best Foreign Language Film. His film "The Life of Wild Matsu" aka "the Rickshaw Man" (無法松の一生, *Muhōmatsu no isshō*) , won the Golden Lion at the 1958 Venice Film Festival, making him one of Japan's first world famous directors.

Mansaku Itami 伊丹万作

Mansaku Itami (1900-1946) was considered a member of the "Talented Directors" group, as besides being a director, he was also a writer. He even joined a film company as an actor in 1927. In 1928, he participated in Chiezō Kataoka's filmmaking as the associate director and the playwright. In the same year, he made his directorial debut "Adauchi Ruten" (仇討流転). His classics "The Peerless Patriot" (国士無双, *Kokushi musō*) and "Capricious Young Man" (赤西蠣太, *Akanishi kakita*) soon followed.

Itami's films are often light and humorous yet slightly satirical underneath. His jidaigekis did not have the sense of belonging in groups often seen in other films. They also did not focus on fight scenes. His samurai characters not only lack heroic qualities, but often are burlesqued as clumsy buffoons.

In 1938, he remade Vicotor Hugo's "Les Miserables" and named it Kyojin-den. This film boldly had actors speak English in dialogs and Japanese subtitles were used. Unfortunately, this ambitious and creative piece eventually was not well received in the film industry, due to the negative influence from the lead actor Denjirô Ôkôchi (大河内傳次郎) whose reputation was worsening. Since then, Itami fell ill and no longer directed. However, later on he wrote screenplays Rickshaw Man (無法松の一生, *Muhōmatsu no isshō*) and "Children Hand in Hand" (手をつなぐ子ら, *Te o tsunagu kora*), both of which were made into films by Hiroshi Inagaki (稲垣浩).

Itami passed away at the age of 46. As a side note, his son Itami Jūzō (伊丹十三) also became a famous director in Japan.

Chapter 3 World War Two Period 1939-1945

1. Film Features of World War Two, Japan

In 1937, Japan attacked China. As the homeland of Japan slowly got dragged into war, the film industry was inevitably involved and affected. After the Pearl Harbour attack on America, Japan was completely sucked into the war.

In 1941, Japan produced 500 films, only second in the world to America. However, by the end of World War II, its annual film production fell to only 26 in 1945. After years of war, the homeland of Japan was wrecked and destroyed; the survival of the film industry naturally became more and more difficult.

The very first impact World War II had on Japan would be the film law formulated in 1939. Though there was a film inspection system before the war, this new film law, modeled after Nazi Germany's, gave the state more control over the film industry. A strict quota system was adopted in film production and distribution. Directors and actors all had to go through a qualification registration system and the screenplays must be censored right from the beginning. After the passing of the film law, many of those against the law were put into prison.

As the war pushed further on, Japan's imported goods and materials became more and more scarce, and the essential negatives needed in filmmaking became rare and expensive. Imported Eastman Kodak film was already impossible to get; domestically produced film became official military material and its civil use was strictly regulated.

Therefore, the Imperial General Headquarters controlled several of the key elements required in filmmaking.

During these years, if any film studio or film professional wished to continue to further their career in the film industry, the easiest was to make war movies for the military. Amongst these, there were both feature films and documentaries, the goals of which were to stimulate the fighting spirit and improve the morale of soldiers on one hand, and to advocate jingoism at home on the other. Some famous directors like Kenji Mizoguchi (溝口健二) and Kajiro Yamamoto (山本嘉次郎) directed their wartime films in the context. Some other famous directors including Yasujiro Ozu (小津安二郎) and Sadao Yamanaka (山中貞雄) even joined the army themselves.

As for film studios, Toho actively responded to the requirements of the army, invested in making wartime films, thus obtaining vigorous support from the army. They adopted the latest aerial photography technique to project the army's vigor and splendor. Contrastingly, without colluding with the army, Shochiku also made it through this dismal period.

In the meantime, Japan's filmmaking system reached its overseas colonies. Many film studios were established in China, Taiwan and Korea. Films that came from these studios were almost all jingoist propaganda, with a small portion contributed to the popularization and education of Japanese culture in colonies.

This period was also considered the darkest in Japan's film industry, where artists had neither time nor space to be creative and were unable to express their own thoughts. The whole film industry became just another part of a crazy machine, mechanically creating another product for the war.

2. Emerging Talents: Akira Kurosawa 黒澤明 and Keisuke Kinoshita 木下惠介

During this period, many Japanese directors who were unwilling to be involved in making wartime films mostly chose to avoid reality and war-related films; instead, they opted to film jidaigekis. Directors like Hiroshi Inagaki (稲垣浩) and Masahiro Makino (マキノ雅弘) even filmed several of their representative works during this time.

In this darkest period, two significant directors came into play and brought fresh air into the film industry. The emergence of these two directors was later proven to have a decisive effect on Japanese films: Akira Kurosawa and Keisuke Kinoshita.

Akira Kurosawa (1910-1998) was born in Tokyo. He loved drawing since he was young and he even aimed to be an artist. However, it was not easy to be an artist at the time. He was accidentally recruited into PCL in 1934 and later became the assistant director of Kajiro Yamamoto (山本嘉次郎). The first few years after he joined the film industry, he learned the different filming techniques from Kajiro and also worked on his own screenplays, which earned recognition from the industry after their release.

In 1943, Kurosawa finally obtained his first directing opportunity in "Sanshiro Sugata" (姿三四郎, a.k.a. Judo Saga) which was based on a judo novel. Japan at the time was deep in war and films were still going through stringent inspection and limitation. Kurosawa craftily selected traditional themes that had little to do with the real issues. It not only successfully passed the screenplay inspection, but also did not fall into the set pattern of fighting themes common in works of the time. Zen enlightenment was easily seen in this maiden film of Kurosawa's. The hero of this was a young man who understood the truth of life through judo training. Kurosawa's use of fast-paced short shots and splendid editing skills left everlasting memories on people. "Sanshiro Sugata", both entertaining and philosophical, earned critical praise and enjoyed success in the box office, setting the stage for Kurosawa's leading role in Japanese and world cinema.

In the same year, another master director Keisuke Kinoshita made his directorial debut with "The Blossoming Port" (花咲く港, *Hanasaku minato*). Kinoshita shared similar experience with Kurosawa in the beginning of his film career. He joined Shochiku Kamata Studio in 1933 and became the assistant director for both Yasujiro Shimazu (島津保次郎) and Kozaburo Yoshimura (吉村公三郎). "The Blossoming Port" is a comedy that portrays two conmen who come to defraud residents of a port town in Kyushu Island: claiming their ship company failed in business and getting people to purchase their company stock. They eventually were moved by the residents' kind-heartedness, patriotism and human kindness and reformed themselves onto the right path. It is worth mentioning that the characters in the film were all unique and departed from convention. Audiences could clearly see Kinoshita's hallmark style: the alternation between joy and grief in real life. His sincere and touching narrative skills in expressing characters' emotions were praised by the public. With this film, Kinoshita won the New Director of the Year award at the end of that year.

Chapter 4 Post-war Golden Age 1945-1960

1. Post-war Censor System and Mechanism

In August of 1945, after Japan surrendered unconditionally to the Allies, the literal and figurative clouds of World War II finally dissipated. Since then, Japan entered a special period where the Allies, headed by America, in fear of Japan starting another war, took control of the country until 1952, and began its reconstruction.

Since October of 1945, Japan's film industry was under the management of the Civil Information and Education (CIE) section bureau under the Supreme Commander of the Allied Powers. To some extent, CIE took over from Japan's Imperial General Headquarters and gained absolute control over the film industry. All films of the period were required to submit their production plan and screenplay to CIE for inspection and only after obtaining a shooting permit could they start filming.

CIE's standards were not guided by the militaristic jingoism of wartime, but rigorously disseminated America's freedom and democracy. In the meantime, the extremes such as jingoism, feudal loyalty, worship of violence, advocacy of suicide and revenge were firmly banned. CIE also further censored any thoughts or concepts on negative portrayals of America. As America was the enemy of Japan at wartime, the Japanese public often rejected overt messages extolling America's concept of individualism and freedom; therefore, all screenplays with this rejection sentiment would not pass. Correspondingly, CIE highly promoted films that reflected on Japan's jingoism; in this context, Akira Kurosawa and Tadashi Imai (今井正) respectively filmed classics "No Regrets for My Youth" (わが青春に悔なし, *Waga seishun ni kuinashi*) and "Blue Mountain Range" (青い山脈, *Aoi sanmyaku*).

In addition, during the first few postwar years, CIE also focused on censoring leftist thought, as the land reform and disbandment of financial magnates were considered somewhat communist. At the same time, under the influence of leftists, the Toho Strike took place, which caused quite a shock in the film industry.

As mentioned previously, Toho worked closely with the Imperial Army General Headquarters at wartime and people started to investigate Toho for its war responsibilities. As Toho adopted an open management policy during wartime, it took in many leftists; therefore, its labor union became the primary battleground when the investigation of war responsibilities started. Other than war responsibilities, the union demanded to be a part of Toho's full management and operation, which was sternly rejected. Afterward, the union split into two sides. The older directors and actors withdrew from the union and started their own company, New Toho in 1947. By 1948, the conflict between Toho and the labor union worsened and got out of hand. Many of the staff were laid off and the labor union took over the studio, starting a seemingly endless strike. This was the first major post war leftist movement and was eventually resolved by the American army.

After this strike, CIE started a large-scale communist purge. Many leftist directors like Tadashi Imai (今井正) and Satsuo Yamamoto (山本薩夫) were expelled from the film industry. Their creative work went underground, and ended up being the genesis of Japan's independent film industry.

In 1951, the Peace Treaty of San Francisco was signed; the U.S Occupation ended and Japan's freedom was restored.

2. Stepping on the World Stage – Winning in International Film Festivals

Japan's economy slowly recovered under the few years' of Allied occupation; its film industry also recovered and got back on the path towards the world stage.

It all began in 1950 with Akira Kurosawa's "Rashomon" (羅生門) being sent to the Venice Film Festival and surprisingly winning the Golden Lion Award. This was the first time for a Japanese film to win the highest title in an international film festival, thus drawing the attention of the world's film audiences to this previously mysterious far eastern nation. Rashomon's win also provoked enormous nationwide sensation in Japan. Japanese filmmakers, for the first time, realized that their own films could also obtain the highest world recognition. For the Japanese people who were in dire need of rebuilding their confidence post war, this event itself was considered the symbol of Japan recovering its power and status, and Director Akira Kurosawa was considered a national hero.

The next few years saw many Japanese films sent for consideration in international film festivals. Those films did not fail expectations and constantly won awards. Kenji Mizoguchi's "The Life of Oharu" (西鶴一代女, *Saikaku ichidai onna*), "Tales of Moonlight and Rain" (雨月物語, *Ugetsu monogatari*) and "Sansho the Bailiff" (山椒大夫, *Sanshō dayū*) continuously won awards in Venice between 1952 and 1954. Teinosuke Kinugasa's "Gate of Hell" (地獄門, *Jigokumon*) also won an award in the 1954 Cannes Film Festival and the Academy Award for "Best Foreign Language Film". Soon afterwards, Hiroshi Inagaki's "Samurai I: Musashi Miyamoto" (宮本武蔵) also won the Academy Award for "Best Foreign Language Film".

Japanese films kept winning awards one after another, which was a new phenomenon. Looking back at this incredible period, one can clearly see the originality in these award-winning films. However, there were also other special reasons.

Firstly, this group of films is all period drama. These jidaigekis with their rich content in far eastern traditions satiated the appetite of western audiences and film critics for the new and exotic. Secondly, "the director is the author of the film" concept, advocated in the 1950's French "Cahiers du cinéma" (translated as "The policy of authors"), spread all around the world. This director-author philosophy augmented the director being the core of creativity. Since Japan's film studios have always adopted the director management system, it predetermined the author quality in the group of outstanding Japanese directors. Furthermore, Masaichi Nagata (永田雅一) from Daiei Motion Picture Company had a bold sense of management. He was the first producer of films rich in far eastern traditions and entered his films in international film competitions, attempting to infiltrate the international film market.

At any rate, this award-winning wave opened Japan's film door to the world. From then on, more and more audiences started to pay close attention to and unearth the values and essences in Japanese films. Japan's film industry thus entered into a new chapter, reaching for its highest level.

3. World's Kurosawa, World's Mifune

World's Kurosawa

Kurosawa's debut "Sanshiro Sugata (a.k.a. Judo Saga)" already showed Akira Kurosawa's directorial talent. After several renowned realistic films such as "Drunken Angel" (酔いどれ天使, *Yoidore tenshi*) and "One Wonderful Sunday" (素晴らしき日曜日, *Subarashiki nichiyōbi*) in the 1940s, Kurosawa's "Rashomon" won the grand prize in Venice, which spurred his production in the 1950s and led to many more great works.

"Rashomon" was adapted from Ryūnosuke Akutagawa's (芥川 龍之介) novels "Rashomon" (羅生門) and "In a Grove" (藪の中, *Yabu no naka*). It centered on a murder case in which different characters had alternative versions of what had happened, further complicating the mystery. The film not only is refreshing in its superb filming techniques and editing skills, but also manifests the ugliness of human nature and reveals the unknown and untrustworthy. From then on, similar stories are often called Rashomon stories.

In 1952, Akira Kurosawa quickly filmed another excellent realist film "To Live" (生きる, *Ikiru*). Takashi Shimura (志村喬) played a cancer-ridden bureaucrat on his quest for the value of life. Through Shimura's most outstanding performance, the whole film vividly and strategically captured the corruption and decadence of the modern world, fiercely attacking the selfish, the numb and the decadent, yet ending it with an incredible humanitarian sublimation.

Kurosawa's 1954 epic jidaigeki "Seven Samurai" (七人の侍, *Shichinin no samurai*) was a production that required, at the time, the highest production cost, as well as the most complicated and meticulous filmmaking skills. It not only was the highest-grossing movie in Japan, but also became one of the greatest and most monumental works ever made in Japan, or even around the world. Its second-to-none charm resulted from its vigorous editing and splicing skills, and Kurosawa's explorations on the characteristics and nature of samurai and villagers in traditional Japanese society. With its rich and thought-provoking content, this film can certainly be considered one of the greatest works of all times.

After "Seven Samurai", Kurosawa successively directed "Throne of Blood" (蜘蛛巣城, *Kumonosu-jō*), "Three Rascals in the Hidden Fortress" (隠し砦の三悪人, *Kakushi toride no san akunin*), "The Bodyguard" (用心棒, *Yojimbo*), and "Sanjuro" (椿三十郎, *Tsubaki sanjūrō*) and took his samurai genre to the pinnacle. "Throne of Blood", an adaptation of Shakespeare's "Macbeth" play, constructed a solemn and dignified atmosphere that revealed human greed and desire to the extreme. In the early 60s, he produced two samurai films similar in style and theme "The Bodyguard" and "Sanjuro", concentrating on refining two rogue samurais' stories, steering away from his favorite grand and deep narratives to something lighter in tone. Filled with both humor and self-deprecation, both films seemed to depict anarchy but really were the embodiment of Kurosawa's prudence and wisdom. "The Bodyguard" was very popular in Japan, earning the highest box office at the time. It also had a huge impact abroad, and the Italian director Sergio Leone remade it into the famous western "A Fistful of Dollars", spearheading a wave of Spaghetti Westerns. During this period, apart from jidaigekis, Kurosawa also made new school films such as "High and Low" (天国と地獄, *Tengoku to jigoku*) and "The Bad Sleep Well" (悪い奴ほどよく眠る, *Warui yatsu hodo yoku nemuru*).

Akira Kurosawa is known to the world for his peerless set management skills. His filming of large scale fights and battles is second to none in Japan. Many scenes in his films, later known as "Kurosawa Style" have been constantly imitated and copied. With his deep understanding of traditional Japanese culture and his familiarity with western theatrical skills, he adapted western plays such as "Macbeth" and "King Lear" and successfully transformed the dramatic conflicts into the Japanese society and onto Japanese characters. Kurosawa was great in depicting themes that reveal clashes and conflicts between the human nature and the human soul. Though he used Japanese reality and history, the themes are universal essential ones which human society is unable to avoid: conscience, desire, pretense, greed, fear and humility etc. Audiences often feel his films are elegies of human nature, not just showing desperation, but making people see the light at the end of the tunnel.

Thanks to Akira Kurosawa, the whole world is able to experience the charm of Japanese films and Japanese culture. He also became the first Japanese director held to such high international esteem. Global audiences are all able to find some kind of connections with characters from his films. Therefore, Akira Kurosawa is the "world's Kurosawa", and in the words of Steven Spielberg, the "Shakespeare in the film industry".

World's Mifune

When Akira Kurosawa is mentioned, most people naturally think of his close collaborator of the 20 years between 40s and 60s: Toshiro Mifune (三船敏郎). As Kurosawa's fame and impact continued to grow, Mifune, the protagonist always active in Kurosawa's films, is also called "World's Mifune", alongside with Akira Kurosawa.

Toshiro Mifune (1920-1997) joined Toho in 1946. After starring in his third film "Drunken Angel" (酔いどれ天使, *Yoidore tenshi*) directed by Akira Kurosawa, Mifune sprang into fame. In the next 20 years, he collaborated with Kurosawa in 15 films, until "Red Beard" (赤ひげ, *Akahige*) in 1965. Amongst all of Kurosawa's films during this period, "To Live" (*Ikiru*) is the only film Mifune did not star in. Kurosawa not only was the earliest to discover Mifune's talent and brought him into the film industry, he also truly tapped into Mifune's acting skills. Mifune played various types of roles in Kurosawa's films such as the gangster in "Drunken Angel" that launched his fame; the artist armed with justice in "Scandal" (醜聞, スキャンダル); the dying elderly in "Record of a Living Being" (生きものの記録, *Ikimono no kiroku*); and the executive caught in a conundrum in "High and Low". Naturally, the most well-known to film-lovers is his samurai role in Kurosawa's many jidaigekis. Mifune was able to bring to life not the same samurai, but each one with his own characters. In "Rashomon", he was an unrestrained bandit; in "Seven Samurai", he was the samurai poser villager, both arrogant and brave, yet also timid; in "Throne of Blood", he was the samurai commander heading to his own destruction, bound by his desire. Without doubt, the most common samurai role Mifune had is righteous, awe-inspiring, generous and loyal. Whether the defeated general in "The Hidden Fortress", or the rogue in "The Bodyguard" (*Yojimbo*) and "Sanjuro", Mifune was remarkably true to life. He truly seemed like the best incarnation of Japanese samurai on screen.

For this reason, Mifune continued to play samurai roles that symbolized justice, even when he worked with other directors. His exceptional performance in Hiroshi Inagaki's "Samurai I: Musashi Miyamoto" (宮本武蔵) and Kihachi Okamoto's (岡本喜八), "Samurai Assasin" (侍, *Samurai*) was highly regarded both in Japan and around the world.

After the 1960s, as the collaboration in filmmaking between Japan and other countries became closer and more frequent, Mifune was invited to play the typical samurai roles in western films. Since generals and samurai share many similarities, Mifune played quite a few military leaders such as the famous Japanese Admiral Isoroku Yamamoto (山本五十六) and General Korechika Anami (阿南惟幾).

Unfortunately, the well-known "Mifune-Kurosawa" collaboration ended abruptly after the filming of "Red Beard" in the 60s. Both of them carefully avoided mentioning the reasons behind their rift, thus forever keeping the world wondering. However, it is known that Mifune did try a few more times to work with Kurosawa and Kurosawa continued to praise profusely Mifune's acting skills. It has been widely believed that Mifune was the most talented and electrifying actor of the time, able to bring to the screen vivid lives of a range of characters when collaborating with Kurosawa, yet was somehow unable to achieve his fullest potential after they parted ways.

4. Yasujiro Ozu's Aesthetics 小津安二郎

If Akira Kurosawa were Toho's pillar, Yasujiro Ozu would definitely be Shochiku's foundation. Ozu was already a popular director during the Silent Film period. After a short stint in the Imperial Army, he went back to filming. In the 50s, he established his unique film aesthetics.

Different from Akira Kurosawa, Ozu did not immediately gain world fame; instead, he was slowly discovered by people as time went by and his reputation has recently reached to a new height. "Sight and Sound", the authority film magazine published its "greatest films" of directors and critics for the most recent 2012 polls and the results showed "Tokyo Story" (東京物語, *Tōkyō monogatari*) ranked no.1 in the directors' choice and no. 3 in the critics'. Though this world recognition came in quite late, Ozu was highly regarded in Japan, even far more so than Akira Kurosawa.

Yasujiro Ozu (1903-1963) was born into an influential family and started his film career with Shochiku in 1920s. Apart from his 1927 directorial debut "Sword of Penitence" (懺悔の刃, *Zange no yaiba*) being a jidaigeki, he focused on Shomingeki working class drama with protagonists coming from Tokyo common families.

After his service in the army ended, he started directing again and his 1949 "Late Spring" (晩春, *Banshun*)saw the beginning of a series of great films. The appearance of "Late Spring" signified his matured and refined skills in film. He centered on middle class families in Kamakura and Yamanote and concisely manifested his "Take things as they come" spirit. Throughout the 1950s, Chishu Ryu (笠智衆) and Setsuko Hara (原節子) were both always featured as father and daughter in Ozu's films, with marriage as the main theme. This seemingly unchangeable theme took on different meanings and appeal when depicted by Ozu. In "Late Spring", the stubborn daughter refused to marry, thus revealing this obscure love between father and daughter; in "Early Summer" (麦秋, *Bakushū*), the daughter was quietly choosing the right person to marry on her own. Through Ozu's exquisite depictions of the characters' emotions and subtleties, the complicated emotions and relationships in an ordinary Japanese family are fully displayed to show their volatility and profundity.

In his most famous 1953 "Tokyo Story", he vividly exhibited the gradual and unavoidable disintegration of the big traditional Japanese family system. Through many detailed portrayal, various family members' characteristics and attitudes were truthfully presented. It showed Ozu's regret and helplessness towards this family disintegration.

Japanese audiences are deeply affected by these films that reflect Japan's customs and traditions; they can easily empathize with the characters, and find the plots very appealing. On the other hand, due to the large cultural gap, western audiences find it more difficult to understand their subtleties and charm, ever though they are very curious towards them. This could be the reason behind Ozu's belated international fame.

Apart from Ozu's unique narrative content, another reason that the world is becoming more and more fascinated with him is his original film aesthetics. Ozu would always position cameras at a very low height, only one or two feet off the ground. The camera's special angle is often called "Ozu 18 Degree". He would even use this angle to film characters sitting on the opposite side of the camera on a tatami. In the meantime, Ozu almost never moved his camera. He tried his best to stop any type of camera movement, whether it is to move up or down or track, so that his ideal framing of the shot would not be changed. Characters in Ozu's films also rarely have big movements. They would usually sit quietly on the tatami, or walk slowly down the hallway from afar, lacking any sudden or violent movement. Ozu was also unique in setting his scenes; he mostly only used standard lens and avoided using close-ups.

Ozu's special preference of "static" helped create the most direct impression. These static characters, and motionless scenes, create Ozu's peaceful and restful state. Created by his distinctive filming techniques, his own humanitarian essence keeps seeping in.

On December 12th, 1963, he quietly passed away on his 60th birthday. On his tombstone, only one character was carved, "nothingness" (無, *mu*), reflecting his original philosophy of life.

5. Kenji Mizoguchi's Magnificent Curtain Call 溝口健二

The respectful and prestigious Kenji Mizoguchi, though already at an old age, did not stop working. During these last few years of his life, he created every film like a master and a few of them are considered the most exceptional films ever made in Japanese cinema.

Mizoguchi was talented and creative in filmmaking but quite oblivious to politics, sometimes even seemed rigid and rough. Therefore, he made a propaganda film "The 47 Ronin" (四十七士, *Shi-jū-shichi-shi*), during the war for the military government, advocating feudal loyalism. Mizoguchi's version is one of the most famous amongst all the Chushingura (忠臣蔵) films. Its four-hour-long epic production showcased his mastery of long shots, space continuation, and characters' divine pattern behavior. Unfortunately the most famous scene in the play "the revenge of Kira Yoshinaka" did not appear; therefore, this film is usually not considered a success.

During postwar American occupation, according to the requirements of CIE, Mizoguchi was unable to be creative under the strict censorship system, and continued to artificially force the thoughts of freedom and democracy into his films, which seemed somewhat pedantic.

In the 1950s, Mizoguchi finally found themes that most fit him and created a group of masterpieces. The first one is "The Life of Oharu" (西鶴一代女, *Saikaku ichidai onna*), adapted in 1952 from Japan's classic literature "The Life of an Amorous Woman" (好色一代女, *Kōshoku ichidai onna*). This film strongly denounced the society's degeneration and injustice through the tragic life of an ordinary woman in the old society. Through his unique directing, the film's moods and ideology were all relayed to audiences in the most aesthetic form. It won the Golden Lion award of the year in Venice and remains to be one of the milestones in Japanese cinema.

In 1953, Mizoguchi joined the growing Daiei. His first film there, "A Geisha" (祇園囃子, *Gion bayashi*), depicted the life of a geisha in Kyoto. Mizoguchi rediscovered his familiar geisha world and exquisitely captured the grace and charm of Japan's traditional geishas. The then-unknown actress Ayako Wakao (若尾文子) was discovered in this film.

Soon afterwards, his world-renowned film "Tales of Moonlight and Rain" (雨月物語, *Ugetsu monogatari*) was released and immediately earned remarkable praises. The film was based on a short novel of the same name from the Edo periods. Through traditional Japanese romantic ghost stories, it criticized war and communicated the mentality "the world is like a dream". Mizoguchi's superb filming skills, the camera's smooth movement, and the aesthetic handling of details to show mystery created the mysterious, obscure, sad and beautiful atmosphere that puts audiences in both the worlds of fantasy and reality. Since its release, the film has always been considered the one that best depicts traditional Japanese aesthetics. It also earned Mizoguchi his second Golden Lion award, thus pushing his fame to a new summit.

The enormous success of "The Life of Ohara" and "Tales of Moonlight and Rain" helped Mizoguchi find inspiration in traditional themes. Without a break, he made two more great films "Sansho the Bailiff" (山椒大夫, *Sanshō dayū*) and "The Crucified Lovers" (近松物語, *Chikamatsu monogatari*), both of which followed the theme of "The Life of Ohara", attacking the corrupt and decadent feudal ideology and society. The former exhibited thoroughly oppression the bottom class bore from feudal lords, whereas the latter exposed completely faults in the lack of freedom to love in the old society. Through these two films, Mizoguchi was able to give out a slight message of positivity, sending people some warmth even in these tragedies.

During his last years, Mizoguchi turned his cameras again towards the group he had always been most familiar with: brothel women. His last legacy "Street of Shame" (赤線地帯, *Akasen chitai*) is like a postwar ukiyo-e (浮世絵), Japanese woodblock print or painting) that shows "pictures of the floating world", vividly portraying a group of different brothel women on Tokyo streets playing out their daily dramas during the Diet ban on prostitution.

Mizoguchi is a controversial figure being caught in scandals with prostitutes, which might be the exact reason behind his deepest insight into this unique group's way of life and thinking. They often become his protagonists that offer the most direct route for him to channel his creativity. His long-term concern over women earned him the "feminist master" title. His films directly showed his admiration, empathy, passion and praise of women. These women holding different social status from all walks of life, possessing various personalities, are usually kind-hearted, brave, welcoming, selfless, affectionate and faithful. Through their misfortunes, struggles and rebellion, the unscrupulous and the corrupted are repudiated.

Regarding filming techniques, Mizoguchi's signature is his "one-scene-one-cut" approach, which means he would finish filming all parts of one scene in a long shot. It requires meticulous planning, a strong sense of space, and exceptional control over camera movement, all of which make up into refined and perfect scenes for audiences. Critics have even compared Mizoguchi's long shots to traditional Japanese scrolls.

Mizoguchi's filming philosophy and techniques predetermined the lack of close-ups in his films; instead, most of his scenes were filmed from far away and were panoramic. Though Mizoguchi's long shots started as controversial worldwide, as it differed from the western montage theory, it eventually gained its worldwide fame, after a group of well-known critics in France praised highly long shot aesthetics.

6. Mikio Naruse's Feminism 成瀬巳喜男

Mikio Naruse (1905-1969), Kurosawa, Ozu and Mizoguchi, were considered as the "Four Masters" in Japanese cinema. However, Michio Naruse's fame seemed to lag behind the other three and he received far less attention. Luckily, his unique filming style and ideology have been taken more seriously, as more and more retrospectives of his films were carried out. He himself has become one of the shining stars in Japanese cinema.

Naruse earned a fair amount of fame even in the Silent Film period. In the 1930s, his "Wife, Be Like a Rose" (妻よ薔薇のやうに, *Tsuma yo bara no yo ni*) and "Three Sisters with Maiden Hearts "(乙女ごころ三人姉妹, *Otome-gokoro - sannin-shimai*) further built up his reputation. Unfortunately, as World War Two expanded, his filmmaking slowly came to a halt.

His 1951 "Ginza Cosmetics" (銀座化粧, *Ginza Keshō*) marked Naruse's comeback in filmmaking. Following his familiar theme, this film revealed the life of women who have been changed by their environment. Its success symbolizes his rebirth. Soon afterwards, Naruse found his inspiration in the works of the famous Japanese writer, Fumiko Hayashi (林芙美子). A series of his classic films were adapted from her works. The first one is his 1951 "Repast" (めし, *Meshi*), depicting in a reserved way a troubled marriage without directly showing their crisis. The film's subtle yet smooth expression of the theme was considered on a par with Ozu. His 1952 "Lightning" (稲妻, *Inazuma*) describes a single woman trying to escape from her poor family yet failing her dream due to her unwillingness to leave her mother behind. His 1953 "Wife" (妻, *Tsuma*) portrayed a wife attempting to stop her husband from leaving her for another woman. His 1954 "Late Chrysanthemums" (晩菊, *Bangiku*) showed the lonely and miserable life of four retired geishas in Tokyo. "Floating Clouds" (浮雲, *Ukigumo*), filmed in 1955, marked a new height in Naruse's film career. It covered the love story between a young woman and a married man, which took place during World War two and went on to postwar years. The protagonist Yukiko held fast to her immoral love towards the married man, which often moves audiences to tears. The heartless and faithless man eventually realized his mistake and requited her love right before her death. Amongst these excellent films, Naruse centered on female roles in families, which often had different problems and crisis during postwar years. How to go on with their life and solve their problems naturally became his theme.

"Floating Clouds" is considered the watershed in his later filmmaking career. Since then, his themes switched from families to the war survivors. Different from the many directors who focused on blaming war for everything and criticized World War II, Naruse zeroes in on the true sufferings: postwar life. Particularly to women who lost their husbands, their companions, their material and spiritual losses were in full display. His later well-known films such as "When a Woman Ascends the Stairs" (女が階段を上る時, *Onna ga kaidan o agaru toki*), "Yearning" (乱れる, *Midareru*), "A Woman's Life" (女の歴史, *Onna no rekishi*), and "Scattered Clouds" (乱れ雲, *Miidaregumo*) all centered on such women. Apart from dealing with the suffering and daily struggles, these husbandless women are often given the cold shoulder and treated poorly by their friends and relatives. Not only do they have to support their family, they also must carefully preserve the traditional family relationships. At times, they are even exploited by their greedy and lazy relatives. On the other hand, their emotions are bound by the traditional value of chastity; therefore, they can only bury their true feelings inside and make sacrifices for the happiness of the whole family.

Amongst these films, the most dazzling one is "When A Woman Ascends the Stairs". The protagonist is a widowed bar hostess from Ginza, Tokyo. Though she lost her husband, she cherishes his memory, thus refusing to remarry. However, in order to make ends meet, she had to socialize with many men. Having experienced and seen the world in the most thorough way, she cautiously dealt with everything, yet she repeatedly got treated poorly and even cheated many times. Her relatives wanted money out of her, and some malicious men cheated both money and love out of her. Through this film, Naruse clearly revealed his pessimism and nihilism; he did show some optimism and hope in the end. This film is considered a eulogy and tribute to those who, burdened with their life, still hold the courage to move on.

Among Naruse's later films, one is very different from the rest; it is also the last film he adapted from a Fumiko Hayashi novel, "A Wanderer's Notebook" (放浪記, *Hourou-ki*) (1962). It is a tragic documentary of the author's autobiographic struggle to survive.

Hideko Takamine (高峰秀子), Naruse's longtime collaborator actress, absolutely brought Fumiko Hayashi's talent and arrogance to life on screen. It is considered a work of art.

Similar to Mizoguchi's deep concern over women, Naruse is also labeled as a "feminist". Instead of Mizoguchi's attacking the old society's corrupted system through his protagonists, Naruse exposed practical problems women faced in the new era. Through these female characters, we can see the same qualities Mizoguchi depicted in women: kindhearted, brave, strong, etc. Apart from all these, they also hold the qualities of women in the new era: independent and self-reliant.

Naruse has often been mentioned because of his working class dramas that were comparable to Ozu's. At times, he would even be considered as another Ozu. However, other than the similar themes, the two directors are quite different in their inner spirits. Ozu's materials come from life, yet transcend life, whereas Naruse's are rooted in reality. Naruse painstakingly and thoroughly observed postwar life in Japan; his characters seem to be real people in our lives and their problems reflected in his films seem to have no solutions, just like in our own life. His profound insight into life gave his films the power to penetrate into audiences' hearts. Probably because of this, the famous American film critic Donald Richie regarded Naruse as the director who understood the most about Japanese women and their trials and tribulations.

Most foreigners who know little about Japanese social customs seem to focus more on Naruse's film language. In filming techniques, his is similar to Ozu, as he limited camera movements, avoided unusual filming angles or fast montage, and focused on actors' facial expressions and gestures. Naruse disliked filming on location and most of his plots took place inside, as meticulous lighting and something even as simple as a look that passes between characters could communicate to audiences those characters' moods and minds.

Naruse was a man of few words and could give off a morose impression. It could have come from the fact that his fame and financial achievements were not at par with Akira Kurosawa who also worked for Toho and his popularity and status could not reach the level of Ozu. His feeling of frustration and pessimism partially led to the overlook and oblivion from audiences. However, Ozu has always highly praised Naruse's films. As more and more people see his works, Naruse's values have been increasingly recognized and approved, thus gaining him a higher status in Japanese cinema.

7. Keisuke Kinoshita's Exploration and Innovation 木下惠介

Another key director in 1950s is Keisuke Kinoshita (1912-1998). His sentimental melodramas and comedies were beloved by Japanese audiences. He was one of the most trustworthy directors at his studio; he was also widely commended for his exploration and innovation in many new filming techniques.

His directing career was usually divided into early, prime, middle and late periods.

The first phase would be from 1943 to his 1951 "Fireworks by the Ocean" (海の花火, *Umi no hanabi*). Within these 9 years, he filmed 19 works. During this period, Kinoshita covered a wide range of themes. There were witty comedies like "Port of Flowers" (花咲く港, *Hana saku minato*) and "Let's Toast the Young Lady" (お嬢さん乾杯！ *Ojō-san kanpai!*); social satires like "Broken Drum" (破れ太鼓, *Yabure daiko*) and "Carmen Comes Home" (カルメン故郷に帰る, *Karumen kokyō ni kaeru*); social drama like "Morning for the Osone Family" (大曽根家の朝, *Ōsone-ke no asa*) and "Apostasy" (破戒, *Hakai*); and popular romances like "The Girl I Loved" (わが恋せし乙女, *Waga koiseshi otome*) and "Good Devil" (善魔, *Zenma*). It is worth mentioning here that "Carmen Comes Home" was Japan's first color film. All of Kinoshita's films reveal his artistic quality of seeking the true, the kind, and the beautiful, as well as his humanitarian spirit.

The second phase in Kinoshita's directing career spanned from his 1952 "Carmen's Innocent Love" (純情す, *Karumen junjōsu*) to his 1960 "The River Fuefuki" (笛吹川, *Fuefukigawa*). These 9 years saw 17 of his works. Other than continuing to work on a variety of themes, he focused more on innovations in techniques and perfected his expressive craft. Famous films made during this period include "Carmen's Innocent Love", "Tragedy of Japan" (日本の悲劇, *Nihon no higeki*), "The Garden of Women" (女の園, *Onna no sono*), "Twenty-Four Eyes" (二十四の瞳, *Nijushi no hitomi*), "She was Like a Wild Chrysanthemum" (野菊の如き君なりき, *Nogiku no gotoki kimi nariki*), "The Ballad of Narayama" (楢山節考, *Narayama bushi kō*), and "The River Fuefuki". In "Tragedy of Japan", he used montage alternate editing of genuine news reel footages; in "Twenty-

Four Eyes", he included vivid scenes; in "She was Like a Wild Chrysanthemum", he used misted sepia and an old-fashioned oval frame to portray memories; in "The Ballad of Narayama", he applied the kabuki theater style into the beautiful wide screen visual film; in "The River Fuefuki", he shot it in black and white, yet swathed the lens with color at times in the brush painting style lenses. All of his innovative techniques are greatly relished by audiences. This period was his most prolific, during which he made the most of his notable achievements.

His third phase covered a longer and windier path. He only completed 8 films between 1961 and 1978, 8 years of which even saw a hiatus in production. One of the reasons was that, due to some disagreement, he broke up with Shochiku in 1965 and left the studio to which he had already devoted 32 years of his career. Still, his 1961 "Ballad of a Workman" (二人で歩いた幾春秋, *Futari de aruita ikushunjū*) and 1964 "The Scent of Incense" (香華, *Kōge*) were well received and successful. The former even was nominated for The Academy Award for Best Foreign Film for its excellent love and hate story; the latter, adapted from a novel written by Sawako Yoshi, was the biggest box office hit of the year and was longer than 200 minutes. During this period, Kinoshita was also very successful in TV productions. Between 1964 and 1980, his TV series "Keisuke Kinoshita Gekijo" (木下惠介劇場) and "The World of Two People" (二人世界) both received high audience ratings.

Kinoshita's fourth phase, also known as his late period, would cover from his rejoining Shochiku in 1979 to the year of his death 1998. He made five films in this phase. "Impulse Murder" (衝動殺人・息子よ, *Shōdō satsujin musuko yo*), "The Young Rebels" (父よ母よ! *Chichi yo, haha yo!*), and "Children of Nagasaki" (この子を残して, *Kono ko o nokoshite*) all displayed his strong concern over social and war problems, showing his compassion for all mankind.

As mentioned before, Kinoshita and Kurosawa debuted almost at the same time and spent a similar number of years in their filmmaking career. However, their styles and statuses formed an intriguing contrast. Kurosawa's films could be said to portray men's strong masculine beauty whereas Kinoshita's centered on women's slender feminine beauty. Kurosawa enjoyed international fame yet was not as well received in Japan as

Kinoshita was. Kinoshita, on the other hand, was loved by Japanese audiences for his most typical Japanese traditions and tastes. Shochiku's two most famous film crew groups were actually led by these two directors. Many of the later known filmmakers took apprenticeship with the easygoing Kinoshita: Masaki Kobayashi used to be his assistant, and even Shohei Imamura wanted to become his disciple. Clearly, Kinoshita was highly regarded and very influential in Japan.

8. Four Unusual and Striking Beauties

During Japanese cinema's golden age, an interesting phenomenon occurred: different from Hollywood studios that focused on male stars, Japanese studios used several famous and accomplished female stars as their pillars. These actresses held a high status and earned the title of "Four Divas". They are: Tanaka Kinuyo (田中絹代), Setsuko Hara (原節子), Hideko Takamine (高峰秀子), and Isuzu Yamada (山田五十鈴). Their beautiful images on screen also became a legend.

Kinuyo Tanaka 田中絹代

In Japanese cinema, the name Kinuyo Tanaka is more than a symbol of the highest class actress; it also represents a legendary story. Tanaka acted out over 50 years of women's struggles and twists on screen; off screen her story itself was like a film. Later, a director named Kaneto Shinto (新藤兼人) even wrote a book about her: "Novel, Kinuyo Tanaka"..

Kinuyo Tanaka (1910-1977) was only 1.51 meters tall. She met director Hiroshi Shimizu at age 14 when she was acting. They got married 4 years later. Their marriage ended 2 years afterwards. The one person who helped her obtain fame would be Heinosuke Gosho (五所平之助). Tanaka was put on center stage when she played in Gosho's "The Neighbor's Wife and Mine" (マダムと女房, Madamu to nyōbō), the first sound film in Japan. She also played in "The Dancing Girl of Izu" (伊豆の踊子, Izu no odoriko), a film adapted from the novel of the literary giant Yasunari Kawabata (川端 康成) and considered to be the first idol drama. This role earned her the title of "Shochiku Idol

Actress".

Tanaka was already a star hit in the 1930s; she could be seen in a number of films directly named Kinuyo. Known as "Queen of Kamakura", she owned the Kinuyo mansion in Kamakura, Japan's "Beverly Hill". It was priced at 6 million yen in 1949, approximately the value of 270 million yen now.

Tanaka was most known for her years of close collaboration with Kenji Mizoguchi, during which many classics were produced. In 1940, she first appeared in Mizoguchi's film "A Woman of Osaka" (浪花女, *Naniwa Onna*), whose original negatives have been long lost in the war, and gained Mizoguchi's trust. It marked the beginning of their partnership. Her 1951 "Miss Oyu" (お遊さま, *Oyū-sama*) transformed her and "the Life of Oharu" (西鶴一代女, *Saikaku ichidai-onna*) regained her top actress status and established her typical screen image – a strong and brave woman. As "the Life of Oharus", "Tales of Moonlight and Rain" (雨月物語, *Ugetsu-monogatari*), and "Sansho the Bailiff" (山椒太夫, *Sanshō-dayū*) continuously won awards in the Venice Film Festival, Tanaka's fame quickly spread to Europe and America. She herself became more and more like the brave and strong characters she played, leading her to break up with Mizoguchi and starting her own director career. 1953 saw her becoming Japan's first female director with her debut "Love Letter" (恋文, *Koibumi*). She also played a strong woman's role in Kinoshita's "The Ballad of Narayama" (楢山節考, *Narayama bushi kō*).

Kinuyo Tanaka is regarded as the most skillful and influential actress in Japanese cinema. In 1985, Japan created an award after Tanaka's name, to recognize and reward actresses who have made outstanding contributions to Japanese cinema. The first actress who won the "Tanaka Kinuyo" award was the later super star Sayuri Yoshinaga (吉永小百合).

Setsuko Hara 原節子

Setsuko Hara (1920-) is tall, and physically looks very different from Kinuyo Tanaka. From the moment she debuted, she has been regarded as the representation and symbol of the west, unlike traditional Japanese women. Possibly due to this, she was invited to play a lead role in "The New Earth" (aka The Samurai's Daughter, 新しい土地, *Atarashiki tsuchi*), a Nazi German-Japanese co-production in 1936's jingoist Japan. When the film was released in Berlin, she visited Germany as a Goodwill Ambassador from Japan and met with Joseph Goebbels, Reich Minister of Propaganda. During World War II, Setsuko also acted in films themed in jingoism and the Great East Asia Co-prosperity Sphere. Riding on the support from the military, Setsuko's career reached its new height. Due to her "patriotic" acting roles at the time, she was even considered as their "Virgin Mary" by some Japanese. This part of her life later became her not-so-glorious experience.

After the war, Setsuko transformed very quickly. In 1946, she starred in Akira Kurosawa's "No Regrets for Our Youth" (わが青春に悔なし, *Waga seishun ni kuinashi*), and played the role of an anti-militarist student protestor's wife, who was therefore scolded and even harassed by others, yet continued to champion her husband's cause without regrets. In this film, Setsuko successfully portrayed a strong, independent, self-reliant and opinionated female image, which completely rid herself of her Nazi spokesperson reputation and transformed her into the ideal representative for postwar new women.

Similar to Tanaka Mizoguchi collaboration, Setsuko Hara's fame is inextricably connected to her years of partnership with Ozu. Setsuko first appeared in Ozu's "Late Spring" (晚春, *Banshun*), playing the role of a professor's daughter Noriko. Noriko takes care of her widower father, has a very close relationship with him, and even intends to delay her own marriage for her father. Ozu's simple and plain dialog and picture composition presented the deep and true feelings between father and daughter that thoroughly move audiences. In particular, the scene of their last Kyoto trip together before Noriko's wedding really depicts the sadness before parting and the gentle love of family. Between "Late Spring" and the early 1960s, Setsuko starred in Ozu's prominent works like "Early Summer" (麦秋, *Bakushū*), "Tokyo Story" (東京物語, *Tōkyō monogatari*), "Tokyo Twilight" (東京暮色, *Tōkyō boshoku*), "Late Autumn" (秋日和, *Akibiyori*), and "The End of Summer" (小早川家の秋, *Kohayagawa-ke no aki*), becoming Ozu films' eternal daughter. (Setsuko Hara herself has led a single life). With her classic look and graceful manner, Setsuko has repeatedly given out gripping performances.

Other than the oft-quoted and widely loved collaboration with Ozu, Setuko also acted in Akira Kurosawa's "No Regrets for Our Youth" and "The Idiot" (白痴, *Hakuchi*); Mikio Naruse's "Repast" (めし, *Meshi*) and "Sound of the Mountain" (山の音, *Yama no Oto*); and Tadashi Imai's "Green Mountains" (青い山脈, *Aoi sanmyaku*).

Unfortunately, at the height of her career in 1963, after the filming of "Chushingura" (忠臣蔵) by Hiroshi Inagaki (稲垣浩), she unexpectedly announced her retirement from acting. Since then, she has shut her eyes and ears to the film industry and secluded to a place that often appeared in Ozu's films: Kamakura near Tokyo, thus abruptly ending a beautiful acting career. Her reasons for leaving the public eye have remained a mystery.

Hideko Takamine 高峰秀子

If Kinuyo Tanaka and Setsuko Hara were Mizoguichi and Ozu's favorite actresses, respectively, then Hideko Takamine would absolutely be the Muse of another director, Mikio Naruse.

Hideko Takamine (1924-2010) started her film career as a child star at the age of 5 in Shochiku's "Mother" (*Haha*). The success of the 1938 "Composition Classroom" (綴方教室, *Tsuzurikata kyōshitsu*) brought her added fame.

Her collaboration with Naruse started in 1941 "Hideko the Bus-Conductor" (秀子の車掌さん, *Hideko no shasho-san*), in which she acted naturally as a kind-hearted and spirited young girl. By the 1950s, she starred in quite a few of Naruse's great works. In her films, Hideko has always been the incarnation of new era women: nice, gentle, brave, strong and independent. Her role would take care of the husband and children, run the housework, support the family when the husband is gone, and manage hers and the whole family's life with a man's wisdom and capability. In the meantime, she would be reasonable and fair, gentle and charming, typical of traditional Japanese women.

Apart from her twenty years of collaboration with Naruse, she was also another master director, Keisuke Kinoshita's, favorite actress. She starred in several of Kinoshita's well-received films: "Twenty-Four Eyes" (二十四の瞳, *Nijushi no hitomi*), "Carmen Comes Home" (カルメン故郷に帰る, *Karumen kokyō ni kaeru*), "The River Fuefuki" (笛吹川, *Fuefukigawa*) and "Immortal Love" (永遠の人, *Eien no hito*). Hideko again played the embodiment of a kindhearted, innocent, carefree and progressive spirit. Whether as a teacher who imbues the future generations with traditional Japanese values, an innocent and pure dancer, or a village wife who dares to hate and love, Hideko' roles reflected humanism.

If Kinuyo Tanaka was known for her acting skills and Setsuko Hara for her beauty, then Hideko Takamine was known for both. She played roles of different personalities and temperaments, and even one of a beautiful young girl changing into an old lady. Having worked with Naruse for many years, she was able to master the subtle nuances of women's mentality. Her performances in "Floating Clouds" (浮雲, *Ukigumo*), "When A Woman Ascends the Stairs" (女が階段を上る時, *Onna ga kaidan o agaru toki*), "A Wanderer's Notebook" (放浪記, *Hourou-ki*), and "Yearning" (乱れる, *Midareru*) created new heights in Japanese cinema.

Isuzu Yamada 山田五十鈴

Isuzu Yamada (1917-2012) was influenced by her actor/geisha parents and joined Nikkatsu in 1930. She debuted as a protagonist and played different roles in 15 films in the first year of her film career. Her early roles were mostly in costume drama. Within three years, under the guidance of a number of well-known directors, her acting skills established her as the top actress in costume drama. Those directors would include Ito Daisuke (伊藤大輔), Masahiro Makino (マキノ雅弘), Hiroshi Inagaki (稲垣浩), Sadao Yamanaka (山中貞雄) and Mansaku Itami (伊丹万作).

Kenji Mizoguchi is one of the directors who helped Yamada reach her fame. Her talent was already recognized by Mizoguchi during the Silent Film era and she starred in a number of his well-received films. In the 1930s, she even starred in several of Mizoguchi's most important works. Though only aged 19, Yamada got married and had children. "Osaka Elegy" (浪華悲歌, *Naniwa erejii*) was the first film she starred in after becoming a mother. Its protagonist Ayako Murai has similar personalities as Yamada herself. When Yamada was only 18, she dated Ichiro Tsukita and got married under the protest of her parents. Unfortunately, the marriage failed to make it through 3 years. Mizoguchi actually investigated Yamada's family background and her history before he chose her for the lead role, because he wanted her to play herself in the film. Consequently, Isuzu Yamada put on the most natural performance as a rebel. She freely alternated between a teenager's innocence and a young woman's flirtations, projecting a level of maturity that far superseded her age. In the same year, she starred in Mizoguchi's "Sisters of the Gion" (祇園の姉妹, *Gion no shimai*)and displayed yet again her splendid acting skills. Both of these successful works founded her star actress status.

In the 1940s, Yamada moved to Toho. Her first film there was Mikio Naruse's *"Tsuruhachi and Tsurujiro" (*鶴八鶴次郎*). She played the role of a Samisen player Tsurujiro. Yamada's consummate acting skills put on a full display of the sadness and dreariness of women's desperation and helplessness.*

Yamada turned leftist later on and was one of the main organizers of the 1948 Toho strike, which directly had a negative impact on her film career and drastically decreased the number of films she starred in the 1950s. As the event gradually died down, she was able to get back on track in 1956. In Naruse's "Yearning", in which many other skilled actresses such as Kinuyo Tanaka, Hideko Takamine, Haruko Sugimura also co-starred, Yamada's performance was the greatest. In Akira Kurosawa's "Throne of Blood" (蜘蛛巣城, *Kumonosu-jō*), an adaptation of Shakespeare's "Macbeth" play, Yamada mastered the role of a Japanese Mrs. Macbeth. Her acting in the film was believed to have even surpassed actor Toshiro Mifune's. In the late 1950s, Isuzu Yamada gradually faded from the silver screen. She signed up with the Toho Theater and enjoyed the rest of her life as a stage actress.

9. Other Key Directors

In the 1950s Japan's cinema was in its prime. The film industry's development and artistic attainments reached unprecedented heights. This was made possible not only by several master directors, but also a large number of talented artists who were at the top of their career. Several other important directors will be briefly introduced below.

Tadashi Imai 今井正

Tadashi Imai (1912-1991) was a significant director in the 1940s and 1950s. He was considered Japan's very first independent filmmaker and several of his films provoked strong reactions due to his left-wing political views.

He joined Toho in 1937 and achieved instant fame with his directorial debut "The Numazu Military Academy" (沼津兵学校, *Numazu hei-gakko*). Once World War II broke out, Tadashi Imai was strongly against the military's film management policy that fanatically advocated jingoism; therefore he hardly made any films during the war.

After World War II ended, he quickly returned to directing films. His 1946 "The People's Enemy" (民衆の敵, *Minshu no teki*) revealed the corruption of financial magnates during the war. After the 1948 Toho Strike, Tadashi Imai resigned from Toho. Films he directed during his Toho period were mostly satires with democratic themes. After he left Toho, he quickly directed two consecutive films that were considered very influential. The first one would be his 1949 "The Green Mountains" (青い山脈, *Aoi sanmyaku*) adapted from Yōjirō Ishizaka's novel of the same name. The film depicts a group of young postwar democrats, with Setsuko Hara playing the role of a teacher who put up a vigorous fight against the feudal forces. Tadashi Imai's second influential film after Toho is his 1950 "Until We Meet Again" (また逢う日まで, *Mata au hi made*), which sternly denounced war through a young couple's tragic love story. The scene of the couple kissing through a glass window which caused heated controversy in that year has been considered the very first "kiss" scene in Japanese cinema. Soon afterwards, Tadashi Imai reached his new creative heights and directed great films such as "An Inlet of Muddy Water" (にごり江, *Nigorie*) and "Darkness at Noon" (真昼の暗黒, *Mahiru no ankoku*). The latter was the first film in Japanese cinema to criticize the unjust postwar trials. This series of works was recognized by Kinema Junpo and the two said films were respectively awarded No.1 film on Kinema Junpo's Annual Top Ten List.

Tadashi Imai's films mostly showed his relatively clear leftist views. He boldly looked at the reality and championed the working class. He is also Japan's first director who started to reflect on Japan's postwar responsibilities. Exactly due to his leftist views, he was alienated by several big film makers and was later forced to make films independently.

Tomu Uchida 内田吐夢

Tomu Uchida (1898-1970) was already relatively famous during the Silent Film period, when he made several outstanding films such as "A Living Puppet" (生ける人形, *Ikeru ningyō*) and "Champion of Revenge" (仇討選手, *Adauchi senshu*). The former revealed cruel relationships amongst people and the latter ridiculed Japanese feudal beliefs and bushido.

In 1932, Tomu Uchida left Nikkatsu and founded his own film studio with several other directors. A series of his works from 1936 " Theater of Life" (人生劇場, *Jinsei gekijo*) to 1937 "Limitless Advance" (限りなき前進, *Karininaki zenshin*) depicted lives of the weak and the poor. At the time, Uchida was the rare director who had charisma, ambition and the potential to be a moral pillar. He subsequently immersed himself into realities of the countryside and spent two years on making the famous "Earth" (土) (1939). In this film, Uchida adopted the documentary technique and put on full display the plight of peasants and the corruption of the feudal society.

After World War II broke out, he was sent to Northeast China and continued to make films in the Japanese-owned Manchurian Film Studio. When the war ended, he was detained as a POW for 8 more years, and did not return to Japan until 1954. His first post-war film is his 1955 jidaigeki "Bloody Spear at Mount Fuji" (血槍富士, *Chiyari Fuji*). Soon afterwards, he made a series of Samurai work "Miyamoto Musashi" (宮本武蔵), which was considered by audiences and critics as even surpassing Hiroshi Inagaki's version.

In the 1960s, he shot another influential film "A Fugitive from the Past" (飢餓海峡, *Kiga kaikyō*), also known as "Straights of Hunger". It is a realistic portrayal of postwar Japan disguised in a suspenseful detective story. As the plots unfolded, the evil hidden behind lies and false impressions was slowly revealed. All shots seemed to reflect the hypocrisy and evil of the human mind seen through the director. Its filming techniques had great impact on the later popular detective films.

Chapter 5 New Wave Period 1960 – 1970

1. **Sun Tribe (太陽族, *Taiyou Zoku*) Films**

Just as Japanese cinema reached its new height in the 1950s, the seed of change and reform secretively started to sprout. Postwar Japan rapidly recovered its economy and a special group of youth coming from well-off families emerged. They had been spoiled and pampered from childhood, did not study or work, led a promiscuous and extravagant life, did not follow the rules of the society or traditional values, and treated everything with contempt. They were considered the parasites of the society. In 1955, a well-known Japanese author, the previous Governor of Tokyo, Shintaro Ishihara (石原慎太郎), published a novel "Season of the Sun" (太陽の季節, *Taiyō no kisetsu*) with these unrestrained youth as protagonists, which caused strong reactions at the time. The book instantly gained popularity and earned the highest literary award "Ryūnosuke Akutagawa" (芥川龍之介賞).

Seeing how popular the book was, the film industry quickly adapted it and put it on the silver screen. The result was Takumi Furukawa's film "Season of the Sun", which was an immediate success. Since then, similar films were categorized as "Taiyou Zoku" films.

Instantly, Shintaro Ishihara's novels, "Crazed Fruit" (狂った果実, *Kurutta kajitsu*) was also adapted into film by director Ko Nakahira (中平康). This film continued to focus on "Yaiyou Zoku" as its selling point; it also brought the author's brother Yujiro Ishihara (石原裕次郎) into the film industry. The tall handsome Yujiro was perfect for a Taiyou role. He was flamboyant and had a strong personality. Coupled with his brother's fame, he became the perfect candidate for the role. He rose to prominence with the film and became the idol of many youths. The film also stirred up many controversies, as the plots revealed two young brothers fighting for a married woman, which is against traditional Japanese values and morals.

Several more "Taiyou Zoku" films quickly followed. They are Ko Nakahira's "Summer Heat" (狂戀詩), Kon Ichikawa's "Punishment Room" (市川崑: 処刑の部屋), and Hiromichi Horikawa's "Summer in Eclipse" (堀川 弘通: 日蝕の夏). In the meantime, Nikkatsu adopted "Taiyou Zoku" themes into jidaigekis and furthered its popularity. Thus came Yuzo Kawashima's "Sun in the Last Days of the Shogunate" (川島雄三: 幕末太陽傳, *Bakumatsu taiyōden*).

In reality, there were only a few of these "Taiyou Zoku" films and this type only spanned a very short period of time. They criticized those "Taiyou" youths to some extent; however, as they mainly portrayed sex and violence, they were undeniably somewhat antisocial, which led to vehement condemnations from the public. Still, these films left important marks in Japanese cinema.

In making these "Taiyou Zoku" films, young directors found the motivation and courage to reform the film industry. These director talents no longer settled on the familiar themes in traditional films; instead, they craved to break up the shackles of tradition and longed to express themselves freely, thus creating more and newer forms for the new era and audiences.

As a result, a vigorous New Wave movement in Japanese cinema was being brewed and fermented, just like France on the other side of the world. The leaders of this movement would be Nagisa Oshima (大島渚,), Masahiro Shinoda (篠田正浩), Yoshishige Yoshida (吉田喜重) from Shochiku, and Shohei Imamura (今村昌平), Seijun Suzuki (鈴木清順), Hiroshi Teshigahara (勅使河原 宏) from Nikkatsu.

2. Nagisa Oshima's Rebellion 大島渚

Nagisa Oshima (1932 – 2013) was the most important in the group of young directors. In his first five years with Shochiku, he was involved in making many films and wrote eleven scripts. In 1959, he was unexpectedly promoted to director, thus fulfilled his director dream at the age of 27. His directorial debut "A Town of Love and Hope" (愛と希望の街, *Ai to kibō no machi*) was quite a success. His second film "Cruel Story of Youth" (青春残酷物語, *Seishun zankoku monogatari*) came out the next year. It depicted the new generation of youth by pinpointing their knowledge of and attitudes towards their own youth, love, student movements and the overall society, thus garnering significant applause. This film has been considered the beginning of Japanese cinema's New Wave Movement.

Nagisa Oshima's personal involvement in several student movements involuntarily prompted him to focus on this student theme. His representative work in 1960: "Night and Fog in Japan" (日本の夜と霧, *Nihon no yoru to kiri*) directly displayed such a student movement in Japan. It naturally showed Nagisa Oshima's leftist thoughts. As it was released in the middle of a political movement in Japan, it was forced to be withdrawn from circulation by Shochiku. Oshima simply left Shochiku in response and launched his own independent production company.

No longer controled by Shochiku studio, Nagisa Oshima could now create more freely. In 1968, he made three films in succession: "Death by Hanging" (絞死刑, *Kōshikē*), "Three Resurrected Drunkards" (帰って来たヨッパライ, *Kaette kita yopparai*), and "Diary of a Shinjuku Thief" (新宿泥棒日記, *Shinjuku dorobō nikki*), which brought fresh air into Japanese cinema. These films could be obscure at times, but are all profoundly thought provoking. They are political and include many innovative filming techniques. Oshima's films mostly use the postwar historical development as the theme and distill Oshima's opinion towards Japanese ethnicity, and his reflection of and criticism towards Japanese traditions, including traditions in cinema.

The 1970s saw Oshim's works becoming more international and covering more themes. In 1976, he filmed his most well-known and most controversial work "In the Realm of the Senses" (愛のコリーダ, *Ai no corrida*). Oshima used unusually bold methods to express sex in this French invested erotic film. Though the plot developed in a simple straightforward way, the artistic expression methods were in no way ordinary. He often used live theater scenes, intentionally distancing audiences from the play, therefore allowing them to watch the performance. In the meantime, he required all actors to be as true as they could be, even directing the two protagonists to "perform" real intercourse. At the end of the film, when the hero and heroine were indulged in their crazy sex act, the heroine strangled the hero with a rope and even severed the hero's penis. This daring take left many speechless. However, the film did not intentionally treat sex as erotic, nor did it use it as a gimmick to hype up the commercial success. Instead, love and sex were revealed as the uncontrollable destructive force, showing the director's desire to break free from all restraints and shackles. Soon afterwards, he made the companion film "Empire of Passion" (愛の亡霊, *Ai no Bōrē*), which won the 1978 Cannes Film Festival award for best director, thus establishing his international fame.

3. Shohei Imamura's Desire 今村昌平

Shohei Imamura (1926 – 2006) was once Yasujiro Ozu's assistant director; he also assisted Yuzo Kawashima (川島雄三) in film making and wrote the script for "Sun in the Last Days of the Shogunate". His directorial debut "Stolen Desire" (1958) (盗まれた欲情, *Nusumareta yokujō*) received much attention. His 1961 "Pigs and Battleships" (豚と軍艦, *Buta to gunkan*) portrayed in manga form an American military base in Japan and displayed his talent in satirical comedy. In 1963, he wrote and directed an important film "The Insect Woman" (にっぽん昆虫記, *Nippon konchūki*). It portrayed the life of a country woman. Born as an illegitimate child, she was always treated roughly and coldly by others. She tried to make a living in Tokyo but ended up working as a prostitute, continuing to be cheated and exploited. Later she managed to open her own brothel, yet treated her prostitutes even worse than how she herself was treated and she ended up going to jail. The film was interwoven with the real historical background between 1918 and 1962, making the characters seem shockingly real. It marked the beginning of Imamura's in-depth exploration of Japanese traditions. His later films such as "Unholy Desire" (赤い殺意, *Akai satsui*), "The Pornographers" (エロ事師たちより　人類学入門, *Erogotoshitachi yori jinruigaku nyūmon*), "The Profound Desire of the Gods" (神々の深き欲望, *Kamigami no fukaki yokubō*) continued to delve into the same themes: some portrayed deep-rooted bad habits of Tokyo's working class; more explored urban customs; some reflected conflicts between the new and traditional culture; others showed clashes between life and death.

In 1966, he filmed an experimental documentary named "A Man Vanishes" (人間蒸発, *Ningen jōhatsu*). It used documentary techniques such as interviews and live shots to investigate what happened to a man who had vanished. As the investigation furthers, the truth seems to be further away. Not only is the whereabouts of the man unknown, it is also uncertain whether he is dead, and if so, whether he has been murdered. More surprisingly, the man the investigation involves seems completely different from what his family or friends know. Instead of being the honest and kind man as they thought, the vanished seems to be a snob indulged in women and money. At the end of the film, through opening and removal of backdrops, the original live shots turned out to be filmed on set. This unique film profoundly presented the relationship between reality and fiction, even leading audiences to bring the actual film itself into question.

Shohei Imamura's films often display fully on screen the most original desire in human nature, which to Imamura, is similar to animal instincts. Imamura has said that he was most interested in "the lower class and the lower body". In his films, the low-class characters always directly and rudely exhibit their greed and sexual desire. They seem to have no concepts of reputation or justice, but simply seek material fulfillment and sexual indulgence. The most typical one would be the heroine in "The Insect Woman". His mentor Ozu once was even repulsed to ask, "Why are you always filming these maggot-like people?" His answer was, "I will always be writing about maggots, until I die." Imamura indeed followed this and continued to do the same in his series of works "Vengeance is Mine" (復讐するは我にあり, *Fukushū suru wa ware ni ari*), "The Ballad of Narayama" (楢山節考, *Narayama bushiko*), and "The Eel" (うなぎ, *Unagi*).

4. Hiroshi Teshigahara and Kōbō Abe's Existentialism 勅使河原宏と安部公房

Hiroshi Teshigahara (1927-2001), son of an ikebana (生け花, *living flowers*) artist, originally studied painting. Several films he made in the 1960s displayed his rich imagination as a graphic designer and his talent as a silver screen artist. Many of his most famous films are adaptations of the famed author Kōbō Abe's work and explore self-identity in different ways.

Teshigahara's most well-known films "Pitfall" (おとし穴, *Otoshiana*), "Woman in the Dunes" (砂の女, *Suna no onna*) and "The Face of Another" (他人の顔, *Tanin no kao*) were all adapted from Kōbō Abe's original novels. His directorial debut "Pitfall" is a historical fantasy that experimented on the fusing of ghosts and reality. It narrated the story of a murdered miner ghost that wandered around seeking the truth behind his murder. Teshigahara's more well-known "Woman in the Dunes", also has a fantasy theme. A widow and a trapped entomologist keep digging sand in order to save themselves from the advancing dunes. This existential story is in essence, similar to the myth of Sisyphus, who is condemned by the gods to spend eternity rolling a boulder to the top of a hill, only to see it roll back down. It reveals the absurdity and futility of human existence and is also a poetic deconstruction of the modern world that advocates rationality. Another famous work of his is "The Face of Another". In this film, the protagonist whose face got burnt received a new face through surgery, which resulted in identity change and confusion. It solemnly presented and explored the philosophical questions of identity and existence.

As mentioned earlier, the charm of Hiroshi Teshigahara's films mostly came from Japanese literary giant Kōbō Abe's existential novels. Abe was deeply influenced by western modern literature, especially Franz Kafka, James Joyce, Fyodor Dostoyevsky. His works tend to explore issues in identity and its loss, society and freedom, alienation and assimilation, and express the gloom and depression of modern characters. The difference between Hiroshi Teshigahara and other New Wave directors lay in the fact that, even though they all explore the identity issue, Teshigahara did not include any political background into his films, thus leaving his films as purely philosophical ruminations.

It must also be mentioned here the importance of the Art Theatre Guild's (ATG) assistance to Teshigahara. ATG was established in 1952 to specialize in releasing artistic films and showing foreign films that are not box hits. It is now the Shinjuku Bungaku Theater. "Pitfall" was ATG's first release of a Japanese film made in its homeland. ATG later created a "10 Million Yen Film" system to fund talented directors who are short on capital, having far-reaching effect in Japanese cinema in the 1960s. Directors such as Nagisa Oshima and Shohei Imamura all benefited.

5. Yasuzo Masumura's Reform 増村保造

Yasuzo Masumura (1924-1986) studied under Italian neorealism master filmmaker Roberto Rossellini at the Cinematography Experimentation Center in Rome, Italy. After his return to Japan, he worked as both Kenji Mizoguchi's and Kon Ichikawa's assistant director. Having had an overseas education, he criticized many aspects of Japanese cinema and considered Japanese films at the time to be too emotional and lacking real conflict.

Once he started directing films on his own, he quickened the pace of films through fast editing, which was entirely different from traditional films. In his directorial debut "Kisses" (くちづけ, Kuchizuke), he enthusiastically portrayed Japanese women as independent entities with desires, just like Italian women.

A series of his outstanding works were products of collaboration with the increasingly popular and sexy actress Ayako Wakao (若尾文子). Their first film together "The Blue Sky Maiden" (青空娘, *Aozora musume*) carried on the style in "Kisses"; Ayako Wakao enlightened audiences with the vigorous youth she embodied in her character. Masumura and Wakao's collaboration continued for more than a decade and led to a large quantity of films. Some believed the importance of Wakao to Masumura would be comparable to that of Marlene Dietrich to Josef von Sternberg.

Many of Masumura's films concentrated on entangling, perplexing yet fascinating sex-related themes. He is one of the earliest Japanese directors to confront the topic of sexual repression in Japanese society. In his films with Wakao "Tattoo" (刺青, *Irezumi*) and "Red Angel" (赤い天使, *Akai tenshi*), Wakao's charming and sensual beauty elaborated this theme. Some critics believed their collaborative films were a sex enlightenment for Japan.

His best works are actually the lesser known "Seisaku's Wife" (清作の妻, *Seisakunotsuma*) and "A Wife Confesses" (妻は告白する, *Tsuma wa kokuhaku suru*). The former depicted a woman who acted on her own; it criticized jingoism and patriarchal ideology through her crazy behavior in pursuing her love. The latter amplified to the extreme the contributions and sacrifices a woman is willing to make in the name of love, even to the extent of overstepping the limits of laws and morals. Ayako Wakao who played the role of protagonists in both films, delivered her best acting skills and amazed audiences.

During Masumura's entire film career, he kept on trying new themes and styles and covered a large number of materials and genres that few others could ever reach. Possibly due to this, he also lacked clear individual characteristics and failed to leave a typical impression on researchers. The quality of his films also varied. However, his exploration on new filming forms and techniques undoubtedly had a huge impact on Japanese cinema.

6. Original Kihachi Okamoto 岡本喜八

In the 1960s, there was a director who neither belonged to the category of the traditional master directors of the 40s and 50s, nor to the New Wave group. This is director Kihachi Okamoto who achieved great heights in filmmaking with his unique and original style.

Kihachi Okamoto (1923-2005) joined Toho in 1943, yet got enlisted in the army the following year, and stayed until the end of the war. After the war, he had the opportunity to direct his first film "All About Marriage" (結婚のすべて, *Kekkon no subete*). This romantic comedy instantly gained wide attention. In the following year, Kihachi Okamoto made "Desperado Outpost" (独立愚連隊, *Dokuritsu gurentai*), which depicted a story of a man going to war to investigate the death of his younger brother, when the war in China was coming to an end. It fiercely criticized the stupidity of Japan's jingoism during World War II and garnered wide acclaims. Its sequels "Westward Desperado" (独立愚連隊西へ, *Dokuritsu gurentai nishi e*) and "Operation Sewer Rats" (どぶ鼠作戦, *Dobunezumi sakusen*) maintained the same level of high quality.

Okamoto's most laudable genre is undoubtedly his chambara films, which are considered amongst the best series of films in the 1960s. These films often show hints of yakuza (gangsters), which came from the series of fairly well-known yakuza films he made in the late 1950s and early 1960s, such as "Tale of the Underworld: the Big Boss" (暗黒街の顔役, *Ankokugai no kaoyaku*) and "The Last Gunfight" (暗黒街の対決, *Ankokugai no taiketsu*). Heavily influenced by American gangsters, both films vividly brought to life the survival conditions of gangsters in the underworld. In his later chambara films, many experiences and techniques in filming yakuza films were naturally applied. At the same time, he often adds a touch of unusual comedy to his chambaras. His characters are not serious, stiff and rigid like the ones in traditional chambaras; instead, they are often dim-witted, loutish drunken ruffians. However, his films are more than the superficial comedy; Okamoto counterbalances them with a solemn or even dark theme. His superb skills lie in his ability to meld gloomy humor and serious dramatic content into a fine balance. For example, his outstanding work "Kill" (斬る, *Kiru*) is a chambara like Akira Kurosawa's "Yojimbo", yet the protagonist is a hippy opportunist who got caught between clan intrigues; both sides demonstrated clumsy and slow-witted behavior that made audiences simmer with laughter. Another example is "Red Lion" (赤

毛, *Akage*) where Toshiro Mifune starred as a man impersonating a military officer helping villagers fight corruption. Though the film did not have many sword fight scenes, through its almost absurd plots, Okamoto was able to deeply satirize the never changing social oppression and empathize with the villagers on their unchanging miserable conditions.

Okamoto displayed even higher artistic attainments, after he eliminated the comedy element from his chambaras. The 1965 "Samurai Assassin" (侍, *Samurai*) is like the Greek tragedy in which the Oedipus patricide theme is perfectly grafted onto a samurai legend at the end of the Tokugawa era. His 1966 "The Sword of Doom" (大菩薩峠, *Daibosatsu tōge*) has been considered the ultimate chambara in Japan. Though the popular novel the film was adapted from already had several versions directed by Tomu Uchida (内田吐夢) and Kenji Misumi (三隅研次), Okamoto's is regarded as the most concise one. The film has been given a dark gloomy overtone, and has been considered as a philosophical rumination on bushido, kendo and humanism. Another phenomenon that is worth considering is that both his yakuza films and chambaras coincide with the crazed Italian westerns on the world stage at the time. It could be said that the great directors from the east and the west think alike, to some extent.

Other than chambaras, Okamoto is also remembered for some of his more serious war films. His 1967 "Japan's Longest Day" (日本のいちばん長い日, *Nihon no ichiban nagai hi*) portrayed what happened on the day World War II ended; from government officials to soldiers and civilians, their different attitudes and moods towards the historical moment were accurately captured on the silver screen. On the other hand, his later "The Human Bullet" (肉弾, *Nikudan*) takes on a fully fantastical and surreal approach and is considered one of the best works in satirizing wars.

7. Masaki Kobayashi's Bushido 小林正樹

Masaki Kobayashi (1916-1996) acted as the assistant to director Keisuke Kinoshita in his early film career. He made his directorial debut "My Son's Youth" (息子の青春, *Musuko no seishun*) in 1952. His 1953 "The Thick-Walled Room" (壁あつき部屋, *Kabe atsuki heya*), based on Kobo Abe's script, already showed his talent. Between 1959 and

1961, he made his close-to-ten-hour-long magnum opus "The Human Condition" (人間の 条件, *Ningen no jōken*), adapted from Junpei Gomikawa's (五味川純平) saga novel denouncing the dehumanizing nature of war. It portrayed a Japanese intellectual who was forced to enlist in the army, faced inhumane treatment, and saw the twisted human nature of war. This film provoked strong reactions in Japan and was often played over the period of one night. It has also been considered as the best Japanese film that showed the most thorough and deepest reflections on World War II. Kobayashi himself also obtained tremendous fame through this film.

However, the best of Kobayashi's works would be the two chambaras "Harakiri" (切 腹, *Seppuku*) and "Samurai Rebellion" (上意討ち 拝領妻始末, *Jōi-uchi: Hairyō-tsuma shimatsu*) filmed in 1960s. The former gives an account of a ronin, a rogue warrior seeking revenge on a powerful clan, the instigators of his son-in-law's seppuku. It has multiple layers of narratives interwoven and overlapping with many flashbacks. With his neat and orderly compositions and photography, Masaki Kobayashi deeply reflected on the values of the traditional samurai code *Bushido*. The film was set against the backdrop of the end of Tokugawa shogunate, a revolutionary period in Japanese history and contrasted the miserable survival conditions of a large amount of homeless ronins with the high status and dignity of samurai in the traditional society. In order to uphold their honor, the declining samurai class in the new era had to choose seppuku, the extreme method, to maintain their reputation. The film thus somberly questions *Bushido* ideals: is the code of honor in feudal society the annihilation and destruction of human nature? With its superb filming techniques and profound ideology, "Harakiri" has been universally considered one of the best films in Japanese cinema. In his later "Samurai Rebellion", he continued his ruminations on *Bushido*, focusing on the loyalty element. The film limned a samurai who was not respected by his daimyo, instead, repeatedly maltreated, therefore, chose to rebel against his lord in the end. In traditional value system, the absolute loyalty is considered the biggest responsibility and honor of a samurai. However, if the lord is already the embodiment of the unjust, should loyalty be still upheld? The film presented such a question and Kobayashi gave a negative answer.

Both of these films thoroughly analyzed and reflected on *Bushido*, which pushed the chambara genre to a whole new level. Another significant aspect lies in the fact that both protagonists are extraordinary swordsmen who faced and beat many opponents yet both of them were ironically killed by guns, the new western weapon. The clear-cut contrast between the sword and the gun foreshadowed the unstoppable change from the old era to the new.

Whether shown in denunciations and reflections on war in "The Human Condition", or the inquiry into *Bushido* in "Harakiri" and "Samurai Rebellion", the pervading and consistent guiding thoughts of Masaki Kobayashi's are eulogies and glorifications of human values. Kobayashi is one of the greatest humanist directors in postwar Japan.

8. Kon Ichikawa's Literary Adaptations 市川崑

Kon Ichikawa (1915-2008) was already well known both in Japan and around the world in the 1950s. His 1956 "The Burmese Harp" (ビルマの竪琴, *Biruma no tategoto*) won an award in the Venice Film Festival and initially displayed his original talent. The film is based on Michio Takeyama's (竹山道雄) children's novel of the same name. It portrayed Japanese soldiers getting along well with Burmese during the closing days of World War II and using singing to resolve an upcoming battle conflict, a world somewhat like in a fairy tale. Ichikawa brought religious concepts into humanism by having the protagonist accidentally converting to Buddhism, thus allowing themes such as redemption, penitence, salvation, responsibility, and appeasing the war dead to unfold at a religious level. His 1958 "Fires on the Plain" (野火, *Nobi*) left an even deeper impression on audiences. It portrays battleground cruelties in World War II Philippines, including cannibalism, and shocked audiences.

After the successive deaths of Mizoguchi and Ozu, Kon Ichikawa was considered the esthetician who gave best expression to Japanese cinema. His films not only embody depressing and mysterious themes, but also possess glaring beauty in their forms. In his "Bonchi" (ぼんち) (1960), he depicted a totalitarian grandmother who made every endeavor to maintain her absolute dominion on a large Japanese family. Ichikawa utilized transnatural esthetics to narrate such a brutal story. In his 1962 "The Sin" (破戒, *Hakai*), he sought after his own stylized expression form in recounting the dark psychological film.

Kon Ichikawa later became the most reliable and bankable commercial genre director; almost all high profile monumental work or masterpieces with official memorial feel were directed by him. His 1963 "An Actor's Revenge" (雪之丞変化 *Yukinohenge*), which has been put on the silver screen many times, brought audiences his new interpretations and presented viewers with many possibilities. Soon afterwards, he was invited to make a documentary on Tokyo Olympics, which clearly revealed his influence and status at the time. This high-cost "Tokyo Olympiad" (東京オリンピック) was presented with creative expressions and exciting photography that focused on many wonderful details of athletes rather than the sports events. His remarkable editing captured a series of close-ups of various reactions the viewers had towards the different games. This documentary has been considered revolutionary.

A thorough review of his oeuvre would easily show his strong interest in Japanese literature. A series of his master works all were adapted from well-known Japanese literature, such as Shohei Ooka's "Fires on the Plain", Junichiro Tanizaki's "Odd Obsession" (鍵, *Kagi*) (1959) and "The Makioka Sisters" (細雪, *Sasameyuki*) (1983), Toson Shimazaki's "The Broken Commandment"(Hakai), Soseki Natsume's "The Heart" (こころ, *Kokoro*) (1955) and "I am a Cat" (吾輩は猫である) (1975), Yasunari Kawabata's "Koto" (古都) (1980), Yukio Mishima's "The Temple of the Golden Pavilion" (adapted into "Enjo" (炎上) in 1958) and "The Hall of the Crying Deer" (鹿鳴館) (1986), as well as Japan's oldest fairy tale "Princess from the Moon" (竹取物語, *Taketori monogatari*) (1987). Through filming these Japanese literary works, Kon Ichikawa has formed his own style and concept in aesthetics. All the beauty of Japanese literature has deeply seeped into the details of his works.

9 More Violent Chambaras

Chambara is an important genre in Japanese cinema that revolutionized cinematic themes and techniques of the 1960s. Its content also evolved gradually from 1950s tributes to Bushido morality to introspection and self-examination of Bushido in the early 1960, to the vivid display of sword fights by the late 60s. Chambaras of this period became more violent, splattering the silver screen with gore and blood. Master swordsmen in films often had to handle many enemies at one time yet always ended up winning, chopping up attackers like a chef does vegetables.

In these films, the protagonists did not strictly observe the code of Bushido; instead, they were free warriors sometimes not even following any clear moral guidelines; they roamed around in society with their super martial arts skills. They could assassinate for survival or money without hesitation; they might also help the weak and the poor on a whim.

Chambaras' transformations took place in form, rather than in themes and ideology, as it was difficult to have a new breakthrough due to its already magnificent history. Chambaras beforehand were like a fierce fire; protagonists both just and evil tended to be filled with vitality and an indomitable spirit, reflecting in-depth ruminations on life and society; on the other hand, chambaras of the period became artistic choreography and expression of swordfights, with directors Kenji Misumi and Hideo Gosha bringing the most influence.

Kenji Misumi 三隅研次

Kenji Misumi studied under famous directors Daisuke Ito and Teinosuke Kinugasa. He directed many influential chambara series such as "Zatoichi" (座頭市), "Sleepy Eyes of Death" (眠 狂四郎, *Nemuri kyoshiro*), "The Sword of Doom" (大菩薩峠, *Daibosatsu toge*), and "Lone Wolf and Cub" (子連れ狼, *Kozure okami*).

Amongst these series, "Zatoichi" has had the most far-reaching effect. It has spanned over 26 films from its first in 1962 to its last in 1989. Among chambara films, "Zatoichi" is a unique sample. The "Zatoichi" series moved through the world of black and white to color films and saw chambara films' transformation from serious themes of exploring human and societal nature to "visual and form first" style of killing like cutting vegetables. Zatoichi, the blind swordsman was not considered the best character in the first two episodes; some might claim the real protagonists were his enemies. Starting from episode three, Zatoichi's character was firmly established. Its later episodes stayed away from traditional chambara themes like responsibility, justice and individual happiness, but feverishly went for entertainment value. The fight choreography of Zatoichi series differed greatly from the traditional chambara films and started a freehand brushwork style.

"Lone Wolf and Cub" series of the 1970s took the sweeping and dicing kills to perfection. The protagonist is a brutal executioner, set up and condemned as a traitor by a government official, and forced to take on his little son and form an assassin-for-hire team just to make a living. Right from episode one, the protagonist took an order to assassinate a child, which was and is still considered as a very bold plot. Its later episodes used new weaponry, unique martial arts elements, and witchcraft as a selling point. All of these, coupled with just enough erotic content, learly show the "cutting edge" chambara perfection of "Lone Wolf and Cub".

Hideo Gosha 五社英雄

Another representative chambara director of the period was Hideo Gosha (1929-1992). He graduated from university in 1952 and joined Nippon Television (NHK) as a reporter and production supervisor. He moved onto Fuji Television as a playwright-director and supervisor, and filmed TV shows such as "Miyamoto Musashi" (宮本武蔵), "Deka" (刑事) and "Three Outlaw Samurai" (三匹の侍, *Sanbiki no Samurai*). In 1964, he remade his TV drama "Three Outlaw Samurai" into his directorial debut, an impressive chambara. In the 1960s, he made altogether 7 chambara films, including some of his signature works like "Hitokiri" (人斬り) and "Official Gold" (御用金, *Goyokin*).

The best of his series would be the 1965 "Sword of the Beast" (獣の剣, *Kedamono no ken*). It continued with the traditional themes in outstanding chambara films like "Seppuku", dissecting and analyzing Bushido from a larger historical perspective. The protagonist, armed with Bushido morals, was tricked into assassinating a counselor, believing his betrayal of the counselor would result in modern reforms, but in fact it was just a power grab by another official. This core conflict was highlighted and strengthened throughout the film, creating an intense sense of tragedy.

After filming two period dramas, "Bandits VS Samurai Squadron" (雲霧仁左衛門, *Kumokiri nizaemon*) and "Hunter in the Dark" (闇の狩人 , *Yami no karyudo*) in the 70s, Hideo Gosha's career took a downturn due to personal problems. The 1982 "Onimasa" (鬼龍院花子の生涯, *Kiryūin hanako no shōgai*) marked his comeback with a new direction. From then on, he switched from chambara to brothel gangster films and directed great works like "The Geisha" (陽暉楼, *Yokiro*) and "Oar" (櫂, *Kai*). These films combined elements such as sexual passion, Japanese classic art, the beauty of Japanese regional sceneries with violence, adding a new light to the old "wild beasts".

Gosha's films are usually filled with large quantities of violence and sexual passion, are fast-paced, have popular plots with distinctive, progressive and passionate characters, and are well liked by audiences both in Japan and around the world. Some even compare his films to a feast for all the senses.

The innovation of Japanese chambara of the period was the last great change to a genre that was already well established. This time was considered chambara's last prime period, as the pure pursuit in form failed to sustain its growth and the 1970s saw its gradual decline.

However, these chambara films have had far-reaching impacts on the world cinema. Many of the later Hongkong Kungfu and action films and American gangster and action films have extracted many elements and techniques from them. World famous directors such as Quentin Tarentino and John Woo have all benefited from the Japanese chambara of the period.

10 Other Key Directors

The 1960s was a time in Japanese cinema where the old and the new came together; the traditional and the innovative were woven into a new cinematic fabric. The older directors continued to create while the new generation of young directors continued to grow. This led to a maturing and expanding growth never seen before in Japanese cinema. The following directors deserve to be mentioned here.

Seijun Suzuki 鈴木清順

Seijun Suzuki (鈴木清順) (1923-) joined Nikkatsu in 1954 and filmed many "borderless" action films in the 50s. They mostly followed the yakuza vengeance formula, adopted the "hard-boiled" style of 30s, 40s Hollywood, but had vibrant colors, more exaggerated plots, and were illogical, sometimes comical and absurd. Though they did not catch audiences' attention in the beginning, he was able to stand out in the early 1960s with his imaginative and non-conformative films.

His 1964 "Gate of Flesh" (肉体の門, *Nikutainomon*) caused an enormous commotion with its bold expressions in sex and immorality. He continued on this path and walked freely between black and white and color films; his exploitation of CinemaScope was also very creative. He successively created great works such as "Story of a Prostitute" (春婦伝, *Shunpuden*), "Fighting Elegy" (けんかえれじい, *Kenka erejii*), "Youth of the Beast" (野獣の青春, *Yajū no seishun*) and "Tokyo Drifter" (東京流れ者, *Tōkyō nagaremono*). In these films, characters' vulgarity and heroism coexisted; facetious fight scenes complemented brilliant plots. It puts audiences in an artificial world while maximizing the effects of exaggeration.

In 1967, Nikkatsu went into a financial crisis. President Kyusaku Hori stated that ""Suzuki's films were incomprehensible. He is not a good director. Showing incomprehensible and thus bad films would disgrace the company", and fired Suzuki, which led to a series of events. Directors, film critics and students held a public demonstration to support Suzuki against Nikkatsu. Suzuki formally took the studio to Tokyo Regional Court, suing for personal reputation damages and demanding compensation of economic loss and a public apology in three major newspapers. Nikkatsu handled the whole lawsuit poorly and was inconsistent: it originally withdrew all Suzuki's films but later started showing his works after "Gate of Flesh". Hori claimed all of Suzuki's films ran at a loss yet could not send a witness to court. After the lawsuit dragged on for three years, Suzuki eventually accepted a settlement proposed by Nikkatsu and received one million yen for the breach of contract. Nikkatsu also published a public apology and removed its release ban on Suzuki's films. It also agreed to let Tokyo National Museum of Modern Art borrow all 37 of Suzuki's films for a retrospective. Unfortunately, due to the lawsuit, Suzuki himself was blacklisted for over a decade, and did not get back to directing until the 1980s.

Masahiro Shinoda 篠田正浩

Masahiro Shinoda (1931-) joined Shochiku after his college graduation in 1953 and studied under famous directors including Yasujiro Ozu. His directorial debut was 1960's "Dry Lake" (乾いた湖, *Kawaita mizuumi*), which portrayed a lonely youth who had participated in a student movement yet abandoned himself to vice. Shinoda was known for his strong background in literature and drama, using a poetic script from Shuji Terayama (寺山修司); his filming techniques garnered a lot of attention in Japanese cinema. His 1964 "Assassination" (暗殺, *Ansatsu*) and 1965 "With Beauty and Sorrow" (美しさと哀しみと, *Utsukushisa to kanashimi to*) completed his inimitable aesthetic sense and beatified Japanese style form.

In 1966, he left Shochiku to establish his own independent production company Hyogensha. Up to this point, he has perfected his aesthetic style and created his masterpiece "Double Suicide" (心中天網島, *Shinjū ten no amijima*) (1969). It condensed and showcased his research in kabuki, his adoption of background paintings and their artistic effects, his experimentation of the use of a kuroko (a stagehand dressed entirely in black), and his portrayal of the fanatic sexual desire as beauty and joy between a man and a woman at the crucial moment of life and death. All of his explorations in cinema art deserved to be recorded in Japanese cinema history. The film was rated as the no. 1 film of the year in Kinema Junpo and Masahiro Shinoda was also rated the best director, winning approval and high regards.

He married the famous actress Shima Iwashita (篠田志麻), whom he cooperated with for many years. The two produced many wonderful films together in the 60s and 70s and were praised far and wide.

Yoshishige Yoshida 吉田 喜重

Yoshishige Yoshida (1933-) joined Shochiku in 1955 and started as the assistant director to Keisuke Kinoshita. He was promoted to director in 1960 and made his directorial debut "Akitsu Onsen" (秋津温泉). It depicted a love affair between a couple from war-time to post war period and boldly captured the psychological activities of the characters' hidden inner world, thus catching the attention of audiences. His 1965 "A Story Written on Water" (水で書かれた物語, *Mizude kakareta monogatari*) sharply investigated incest and mental griminess of the world. He filmed his masterpiece "Eros Plus Massacre" (エロス+虐殺, *Erosu purasu gyakusatsu*) in 1970, portraying the anarchist Sakae Osugi and his relationship with three women. In this film, he navigated between the past, the present and the future and searched for the juncture between sex and terrorism in Japanese modern history. It has been considered extremely inspiring and avant garde.

Yoshishige Yoshida, Nagisa Oshima and Masahiro Shinoda were considered "Shōchiku Nouvelle Vague" of the year.

Kaneto Shindo 新藤兼人

Kaneto Shindo (1912-2012) wrote many scripts for Kozaburo Yoshimura (吉村公三郎) in his early years and later became the assistant director to Kenji Mizoguchi. In the 1950s, he obsessed over the conflict between films' artistic and commercial value; therefore, his works at the time explored on different themes and styles.

When his masterpiece "The Naked Island" (裸の島, *Hadaka no shima*) came out in 1960, many had high hopes on him revolutionizing Japanese cinema. The film gave an account of a poor farmer's family who had to boat to another place to retrieve water to irrigate their land on an island. The whole film had no dialog yet was extremely moving. Without dialogs, it offered audiences myriad explanations: protest and critique of the society, or the mental desperation. To Shindo, it was more important to evoke feelings than telling morals, which was also clearly shown in his other hit film "Onibaba" (鬼婆), which vividly and ironically tells of two women killing others for fun in a remote swamp.

Other than being a director, Shindo was also an outstanding screenwriter. Almost all of his scripts were written by himself. He was known to the world for his shocking documentaries and his often interweaving of documentary imagery with fictional plots. His portrayal of sex throughout his oeuvre also formed his uniqueness.

Chapter 6 Declining and Stagnant Period 1970-1989

1. The Dramatic Decline of the Film Market

In 1960, Japan made altogether 547 films and its film industry was at its height. The number of viewers reached its peak in 1958, with the highest being 1.1billion. However, both the film production quantity and the number of viewers started their gradual decline in the 60s. The major factor was the same as around the world: television was quickly gaining popularity.

Japan started television broadcasting in 1953; by 1959, television sets started to enter homes of the general public. By the 1964 Tokyo Olympics, many families already switched to color TV. In order to compete against TV for viewers and display its unsurpassable superiority, Japanese cinema widely adopted color and wide silver screen technologies to make new films. Regardless of its painstaking effort, the downturn of the film industry was hard to reverse.

Large production companies that prospered in the past found it hard to make a living. Nikkatsu sold its production company in 1969 and even stopped its movie production in 1971. Daiei was able to sustain its growth temporarily, thanks to a series of bold management policies in the 1960s; however, it was unable to survive the attack from the overall decline and was forced to declare bankruptcy in 1971.

Apart from the fact that the film production system was on the verge of disintegration and collapse, the accompanying star system also saw its gradual demise. Film actors no longer belonged to a specific production company; instead, they worked on a contract basis. One after another, stars would even establish their own production companies for their own films. As the film industry was unable to train new stars quickly to fill in the gap, TV stars and singers would take the leap into the film industry. In the meantime, lack of young talent in different fields of the film industry continued to worsen.

The dramatic decline was completely irreversible after the 1970s. The total release of films in 1971 went down to 367, approximately only 70% of the production 10 years ago. Major production companies went down from 6 to 5 and their production quantity drastically decreased from 520 to 160. Out of the 367 films, close to 160, over 40% were low-budget pink films. There were also 48 films made by independent production companies, a seemingly booming section.

2 Nikkatsu – The Erotic Empire

To face the decline, the oldest film studio Nikkatsu became the first to make a revolutionary move. It restructured the company around labor unions, and decided on the route of filming Roman Porno, aka pink films in 1971, which led to its successful buyback of its previously sold studio.

After the reborn Nikkatsu announced its pink film direction, many directors and actors resigned over this change in focus. Therefore, those directors who could not obtain an opportunity in the past were pushed to the front stage, as long as they made erotic films required by the company.

The two most influential directors during Nikkatsu's pink film period would be Koji Wakamatsu (若松孝二) and Tatsumi Kumashiro (神代辰巳).

Koji Wakamatsu 若松孝二

Koji Wakamatsu, one of the strongest directors in Japanese cinema, has been known as the pink godfather. His films covered a wide range of content and dealt with controversial topics. Other than advocating porno, elements such as fate, human nature, politics and violence both shine and obscure his films. His 1965 "Secret behind the Walls" (壁の中の秘事, *Kabe no naka no himegoto*) was entered into the Berlin Film Festival yet caused mixed reactions in Japan; some reporters labeled this event as "Japan's shame". Koji Wakamatsu was not affected by these external factors and continued with his creativity which made his wild style stand out even more. His works at the time were sensational, odd and eccentric, surreal and supernatural. His "Embryo Hunts in Secret" (胎児が密猟する時, *Taiji ga Mitsuryō Suru Toki*) and "Violated Angels" (犯された白衣, *Okasareta Hakui*) were the perfect embodiments of his erotic oddity.

Just like Nagisa Oshima, Koji Wakamatsu used to be a radical leftist. He even followed diligently the radical left-wing organization Japanese Red Army, had a close relationship with the organization's key leaders, and went to the Middle East to make the documentary "Red Army/P.F.L.P: Declaration of World War" (赤軍 PFLP・世界戦争宣言, *Sekigun-PFLP: Sekai senso sengen*) in 1971, showing his passion for revolution at the time. Over thirty years later, he filmed "United Red Army" (実録・連合赤軍 あさま山荘への道, *Jitsuroku Rengo Sekigun: Asama sanso e no doutei*). Though it did not carry as much fervor, it was filled with reflections and lament. The contrast of the two films might shed light on the track of Japan's left-wing movement since the late 1960s.

Tatsumi Kumashiro 神代辰巳

Tatsumi Kumashiro (1927-1995) was the absolute representative of Nikkatsu's pink film period and earned the title, "King of Nikkatsu Roman Porno".

Kumashiro started working for Nikkatsu as Shohei Imamura's assistant. In 1968, he made his directorial debut "Front Row Life" (かぶりつき人生, *Kaburitsuki jinsei*). It told the story of a stripper mother and her daughter; unfortunately, it failed at the box office, leading Nikkatsu to put Kumashiro's directing career on hold. A few years later, he followed the company policies, was given another chance, and he started making pink films. In 1972, he directed his second film "Wet Lips" (濡れた唇, *Nureta Kuchibiru*), quickly followed by "Ichijo's Wet Lust" (一条さゆり 濡れた欲情, *Ichijō Sayuri: nureta yokujō*); both films were very popular. Kumashiro continued to make films of similar themes. Apart from those, he also filmed realistic work "Failed Youth"(青春の蹉跌, *Seishun no satetsu*) that portrayed the ambition and loss of youth. This film was rated as one of the top ten by Kinema Junpo.

Kumashiro was the most successful director who walked between the lines of mainstream and fringe films. Known for his erotic films with enough content that deals with serious and profound topics, he set out to show the Japanese public how to enjoy sex during holidays. In his films, there is always more than one woman; they are all very optimistic and easily succeed in the end. Their existence is magnetic like the earth. Contrary to these female images, all male characters in his films are always melancholy and overcautious.

3. Toei's "Battles without Honor or Humanity"

Amongst the six major film studios of Japan, Toei was founded comparatively late (1951) yet had the steadiest growth post war. With its strong foot in 50s' period films and its success in 60s' Nynkyo eiga (任侠映画) or chivalry films, Toei became the film studio with the most blockbuster potential. However, the countless ties between the student movement and chivalry films predetermined the latter's demise after the former's decline. In due time, Toei introduced action films with yakuza protagonists. These films beautified yakuza characters and its ultra-violent and realistic documentary-like style became the avant-garde of new documentary films. Amongst these yakuza filmmakers, the most meritorious and successful director would be Kinji Fukasaku (深作欣二), the maker of the well-known series of "Battles without Honor or Humanity" (仁義なき戦い, *Jingi naki tatakai*).

Kinji Fukasaku 深作欣二

Right after Kinji Fukasaku (1930-2003) joined Toei in 1960s, his series of yakuza films "Wandering Detective: Tragedy in Red Valley" (風来坊探偵 赤い谷の惨劇, *Fūraibō tantei: akai tani no sangeki*), "High Noon for Gangsters" (白昼の無頼漢, *Hakuchu no buraikan*), and "Ceremony of Disbanding" (解散式, *Kaisanshiki*) were all well received by audiences, reflecting Kinji's directorial talent. His 1972 "Under the Flag of the Rising Sun" (軍旗はためく下に, *Gunki hatameku moto ni*) portrayed a war widow's mission to find out the truth behind the death of her husband, who, as a regular soldier, supposedly executed his superior officer. It was considered an anti-war masterpiece. However, his most important and most outstanding work would always be the influential "Battles without Honor or Humanity" (仁義なき戦い, *Jingi naki tatakai*).

"Battles without Honor or Humanity" was adapted from manuscripts written by the real-life yakuza Kozo Mino when he was in prison. It chronicles a young veteran growing from a street thug into a yakuza boss, which was in reality, 30 years of history behind Hiroshima mafia. Instead of following the usual "fists plus pillows" formula at Toei, Kinji Fukasaku recorded cruelties of yakuza life in a documentary-like style. Its release caused strong reactions which pushed Fukasaku to quickly make a sequel "*Battles Without Honor and Humanity: Hiroshima Deathmatch*" (仁義なき戦い 広島死闘篇, *Jinginaki tatakai: Hiroshima shitō hen*) in the same year. The following year saw three more sequels "*Battles Without Honor and Humanity: Proxy War*" (仁義なき戦い 代理戦争, *Jinginaki tatakai: Dairi senso*), "*Battles Without Honor and Humanity: Police Tactics*" (仁義なき戦い 頂上作戦, *Jinginaki tatakai: Chojo sakusen*), and "*Battles Without Honor and Humanity: Final Episode*" (仁義なき戦い 完結篇, *Jinginaki tatakai: Kanketsu hen*). In this famous series, every character's introduction was accompanied with background information like in television news, along with insertions of subtitles like in documentaries. The dichotomy of evil and good lost its meaning here; what is left is the violent truth behind territory wars between different yakuza families.

Fukasaku's films rarely failed. As a director for his countrymen, most of his works fared well in box office and had a good reputation. Both his yakuza and period films have had far-reaching effect. His 1978 "Shogun's Samurai" (柳生一族の陰謀, *Yagyū ichizoku no inbō*) marked a turning point in his career. After seven or eight years of making yakuza films at Toei, it was hard for him to come up with something new in the yakuza genre; therefore, Fukasaku switched to chambara, which led to great works like "Shogun's Samurai", "Samurai Reincarnation" (魔界転生, *Makai Tenshō*), and "Legend of the Eight Samurai" (里見八犬伝, *Satomi hakkenden*).

Fukasaku continued making films in 1980s. Films like "Fall Guy" (蒲田行進曲, *Kamata koshin kyoku*), "House on Fire" (火宅の人, *Kataku no hito*), "A Chaos of Flowers" (華の乱, *Hana no ran*) all were created during this period. "Fall Guy" dramatized anecdotes that took place in Shochiku's Kamata film studio and brought them onto the silver screen. Behind the façade of laughter, ridicules, arguments and fights, the simple and straightforward tenderness and love were revealed. "House on Fire" narrates extramarital affairs, which have deep roots in Japanese culture, since Japanese consider the forbidden love between men and women as temporary love drifts and floats. This forbidden love is evanescent yet passionate, like fireworks, magnificent yet lonely, with both sides willingly losing themselves in the illicit love.

Kinji Fukasaku's films are not only blockbusters, they are also highly acclaimed for their artistic achievements. His films entered Kinema Junpo's top ten list many times. In his twilight years, he was still able to produce a modern classic "Battle Royale" (バトル・ロワイアル, *Batoru Rowaiaru*).

4. Yoji Yamada– the Sole Support of New Shochiku 山田洋次

As Shochiku's master director Ozu already passed away, and Kinoshita also gradually withdrew himself from creating more films, Yoji Yamada, a director of the new generation who was great at comedies, began to support Shochiku.

During this period, rather than Yoji Yamada himself, it was actually his one series "Tora-san" （寅さん）that saved Shochiku. This famous series titled "It's Tough Being a Man" (男はつらいよ, *Otoko wa tsurai yo*) spanned 26 years from 1969 to 1995. Yamada met the comedian actor Kiyoshi Atsumi in 1968 and wanted him to play the lead role in Fuji Television's "Tora-san" series. The TV version finale ended with Tora-san's death, which caused public wrath; many audiences even complained to Fuji Television. In 1969, Yamada suggested making Tora-san series into films but encountered fierce opposition from the company; however, Yamada eventually was able to prevail and make the film. It was unexpectedly well received, became a huge box office success. Yamada, who never thought of making Tora-san film series, decided to continue with the filming. By the time it reached its last episode in 1995, there have been altogether 48 episodes with Yamada directing all but the 3rd and the 4th; it became the longest running film series in Japanese cinema history. Tora-san series' great performance at the box office ensured Yamada's strong foothold at Shochiku.

Subsequently in 1977, his film "The Yellow Handkerchief" became a classic romance in modern Japan. He boldly chose Ken Takakura, well known for yakuza roles, to play the gloomy and tender protagonist, which was quite refreshing. Yamada's later "A Distant Cry from Spring" (遙かなる山の呼び声, *Haruka naru yama no yobigoe*) also earned high acclaim.

Thanks to his series of populist films, Yamada was well loved by Japanese audiences. He himself has always hoped that his audiences can have fun with his films and he has always emphasized film's entertainment, rather than artistic values. His characters are usually optimistic, righteous, kind-hearted, humorous and human; therefore, he has been considered as the director closest to popular sentiments.

5. The Rise of the Anime Industry

While the film industry went further into a quagmire in the 1980s, a force that was already burgeoning actually started to strengthen and rise at this time. It not only opened up a whole new field in film creation, it also rapidly gained recognition from Japanese audiences in a very short time. It later even became an indispensable force in Japanese cinema and generated significant international impact. This would be the anime industry.

Hayao Miyazaki and Studio Ghibli 宮崎駿スタジオジブリ

Speaking of Japanese anime, Hayao Miyazaki (1941-) must be mentioned first. After college graduation, Hayao Miyazaki joined Toei Animation in April, 1963, as an animator. Before Osama Tezuka established Mushi Production in 1961, Toei Animation was almost the only animation company in Japan that had long traditions in paying attention to films' humanistic qualities. In Toei, Miyazaki met Isao Takahata, his senior and predecessor who has greatly influenced his animation career. During this time, Miyazaki participated in the production of "Wolf Boy Ken" (狼少年ケン, *Ōkami Shōnen Ken*) (Toei's TV anime), "Hols: Prince of the Sun" (太陽の王子 ホルスの大冒険, *Taiyō no Ōji: Horusu no Daibōken*) (directed by Isao Takahata), and "Puss in Boots" (長靴をはいた猫, *Nagagutsu o Haita Neko*).

In 1979, he made the feature anime film "Lupin III: The Castle of Cagliostro" (ルパン

三世 カリオストロの城, *Rupan Sansei: Kariosutoro no Shiro*). Soon afterwards in 1983, he filmed the influential piece "Nausicaä of the Valley of the Wind" (風の谷のナウシカ, *Kaze no Tani no Naushika*). Miyazaki single-handedly directed, scripted, and story-boarded the whole film. Its exceptional storyline moved many audiences and its deep exploration of the relationship between nature and humans earned universal acclaim.

In 1985, with funding from Tokuma Shoten, he and Takahata co-founded Studio Ghibli, whose name came from an Italian reconnaissance aircraft during World War II, meaning "the hot wind from Sahara Desert". Since Miyazaki's father used to work at an airplane parts manufacturing company, Miyazaki has always been fascinated with planes and the sky. All of these contributed to the birth of "Ghibli". Owing exactly to these, many of his later works would consistently contain scenes in the sky with many details on various aircrafts. His next classic piece "Laputa Castle in the Sky" (天空の城ラピュタ, *Tenkū no Shiro Rapyuta*) is the quintessential incarnation. Its rich imagination embodies Miyazaki's yearning for a peaceful and harmonious dream world.

Following "Laputa", Miyazaki's works came one after another, all earning high acclaim. Films such as "My Neighbor Totoro" (となりのトトロ, *Tonari no Totoro*), "Kiki's Delivery Service" (魔女の宅急便, *Majo no Takkyūbin*) and "Porco Rosso" (紅の豚, *Kurenai no Buta*), with their different themes and genres, have all become anime classics. His "temporary retirement" followed the making of "Princess Mononoke" (もののけ姫, *Mononoke-hime*), which created the box office record of Japanese cinema. Its call for attention to nature has also been well received. In 2001, "Spirited Away" (千と千尋の神隠し, *Sen to Chihiro no Kamikakushi*) was released. Even though the overall total box office of the year from Japan's anime industry only reached 500 billion and the usual top box office would barely reach 3 billion, "Spirited Away" actually exceeded 30 billion yen, creating a new record,. This film even won "The Academy Award for Best Foreign Language Film", which pushed Miyazaki's fame to a new summit.

Though Osama Tezuka, not Miyazaki, is considered the father of Japanese anime, Hayao Miyazaki and Studio Ghibli, when compared with other animators, have become synonymous with Japanese anime. This is because Miyazaki not only has been constantly perfecting his skills in illustration and animation, he has also communicated his love of nature and humanity through all of his films. His protagonists are usually naïve, kind young girls who fight hard against the evil forces in a society filled with filth, lies, violence and injustice. They embody the best qualities of the humanity, which is also the most touching element in his anime. His later works reveal a more mature Miyazaki who has had more in-depth and dialectical deliberation over the relationship between nature and mankind. Audiences can easily see through his anime works the breadth and depth of this exploration, which are rare in ordinary anime. Miyazaki's works are more than suited for children, are more than exciting adventure stories, but lead people to more serious ponderings towards life and the world. It is another important factor in the worldwide recognition of his films.

Today's Miyazaki and Studio Ghibli is already a living legend that will continue to bring surprises to the world.

Katsuhiro Otomo 大友克洋

Katsuhiro Otomo (1954-) is another major anime director who rose to fame in the late 1980s. To this day he has created five commercial anime. His best work is "Akira" (アキラ, *AKIRA*), completed in 1988. The most prominent characteristics of Katsuhiro Otomo's works are the portrayal of common heroes and infatuation towards machines.

The heroes in his works are the ones who have transformed from the traditional to modern times. In his heroes, traces of traditional heroes can be seen, as can the regular Joe's qualities that completely differ from those old-style ones. He created four average Joe heroes: a teenage gangster in "Akira", a young nursing student Haruko in "Old Man Z" (老人 Z, *Rōjin Zetto*), an outsider Kenichi in "Metropolis" (メトロポリス, *Metoroporisu*), and Ray, the young descendant of two generations of inventors in "Steamboy" (スチーム ボーイ, *Suchīmubōi*). All of them do not possess extraordinary physical ability, nor do they have supernormal intelligences. In the cases of "Old Man Z" and "Metropolis", they might even be considered as below average. Most importantly, none of Katsuhiro Otomo's heroes fight for the interest of their group, although the group interest is indirectly and passively attended to. This aspect differs greatly from the heroes in Hayao Miyazaki's films.

Katsuhiro Otomo's infatuation towards robots, as shown in his works, is considered a very intriguing topic. This sensitive infatuation, filled with passion, is also accompanied by rational fear, which reveals conflicted feelings inherited from Osamu Tezuka, and is the product of a mixture of modernistic concepts. It has appeared in all of Katsuhiro Otomo's major works. His unfaltering devotion to this sci-tech tool and the eventual unavoidable destruction, as shown in his films, is always the most moving contradiction in his stories and has become his trademark. Since then, this paradox of admiration and fear of science and technology has become one of the most important living themes in all sci-fi products in the world.

6. "Emperor" Kurosawa's Later Period

Since the completion of "Red Beard" (赤ひげ, Akahige) in 1965, Akira Kurosawa encountered difficulties in making new films. His next work "The Town Without Seasons" (どですかでん, Dodes'ka-den) was not finished until 1970, which unfortunately performed poorly in box office. Due to this, Kurosawa could not find funding. Thus, he became very pessimistic and even attempted suicide; fortunately, death did not take away the "emperor" of the film industry.

In 1972, Akira Kurosawa received an invitation to film the Russian film "Dersu Uzala". At the time, Russian film studios were under government control. Working with a group of Russians, Kurosawa finished the film in two years. The film portrayed the story of a group of surveyors exploring the Russian Far East. The film showed Kurosawa's love and fear towards nature and won the 1976 Academy Award for Best Language Film.

Due to Kurosawa's increasingly larger film budgets, he was unable to secure financing for new work in Japan. Fortunately, his international fame helped him. When his fans, new Hollywood directors Francis Coppola and George Lucas, who considered Kurosawa a role model, found out about his inability to secure funding, they began to fund Kurosawa's next project.

This would be "Shadow Warrior" (影武者, Kagemusha), the film that won the Palme d'Or at the Cannes Film Festival. It told about a famous warlord during Japan's Sengoku period and his double, the namesake "Shadow Warrior" who flawlessly impersonates him. The film has surprising and enchanting scenes that make audiences feel the coldness of the world. Those scenes are supremely splendid and seem to transcend the human world; the coldness controls everything, crushes characters, and eventually leads to annihilation.

Soon afterwards, he tried another Shakespearean play adaption. "King Lear" became "Ran" (乱). It narrated a series of changes in events and characters and finally revealed humans' stupidity and ignorance.

In both of these epic films, Kurosawa's unprecedented magnificent battle scenes stunned audiences around the world; behind all of these, we could also see Kurosawa in his later years seemed to hold much more pessimistic views. The tragic endings of both films showed absolutely no hope. This could be the true description of his inner mind after what he has had to go through over the years.

1990s saw Kurosawa filming more relaxed and enjoyable themes until his death in 1998. No accolades can be used too much on this film giant, considering how much he has contributed to world cinema. To all filmmakers of both Japan and the whole world, he is a master, and a monument.

7 Resurgence of Older Generation of Directors

Like Akira Kurosawa, quite a few directors went through a similar situation. Their film creations came to a standstill, due to different reasons. By the 80s, they were able to regain their stage and contribute a batch of works of high artistic standards.

The first resurgence would belong to Seijun Suzuki (鈴木清順). After 10 years of being blacklisted, he went back to work, although his style would slightly differ from his previous works. His new films are more surreal and other-worldly, and considered to be the perfect combination of the epitome of postwar Japanese cinema's concise aesthetics and Baroque spirit. Suzuki turned his attention to Kyoka Izumi, the novelist who has contributed most to the new school drama (*shinpageki*) in Japanese literature. Focusing on the deeply oppressed yet fantastical side of Kyoka Izumi's created world, Suzuki successfully directed his own "film kabuki". Thus came the trilogy "*Zigeunerweisen*", "Heat-Haze Theater" (陽炎座, *Kagero-za*), and "Yumeji" (夢二). Though they were all hard to grasp, when compared to films he directed in the 60s, they reached a new artistic height.

Another director making a comeback would be Shohei Imamura (今村昌平). Unable to secure funding throughout the 70s, with the exception of "Vengeance is Mine" (復讐するは我にあり, *Fukushū suru wa ware ni ari*), he spent most of his time making TV documentaries. His 1983 "The Ballad of Narayama" (楢山節考, *Narayama bushiko*) brought him back to his familiar theme – desire; it put on full display mankind's uncontrollable and most original desire. This film won the Palme d'Or at the Cannes Film Festival. Invigorated, Shohei Imamura kept up his creations into the 90s. His 1997 "The Eel" (うなぎ, *Unagi*) won another Palme d'Or, making him the only Japanese director earning such highly-esteemed world awards twice and garnering him more international fame.

Nagisa Oshima (大島渚), another key member of the New Wave, did not stop his creative work either. His films in the 80s are even more shocking than his previous works. His famous

"Merry Christmas, Mr. Lawrence" (戦場のメリークリスマス, *Senjō no Merī Kurisumasu*) depicted a homosexual love story set in a wartime prison camp for British soldiers during World War II. His "Max, Mon Amour" (マックス、モン・アムール) explored a triangle love story between a couple and an animal, a theme that is even rare in modern days. Both films led to heated debates due to their bold themes; however, it is undeniable that they have very strong artistic appeal.

Kon Ichikawa (市川崑), the frontline director always holding huge commercial success at the box office, contributed the glamorous "The Makioka Sisters" (細雪, *Sasameyuki*), filmed to commemorate the 50th anniversary of the founding of Toho. It is considered a top feast film of Japanese cinema at the time and only a director like Kon Ichikawa could be trusted and assigned for the job. This film was adapted from "Light Snow" (*Sasameyuki*), the famous work of a literary giant Jun'ichirō Tanizaki (谷崎潤一郎). Its scenes fully displayed Japan's cultures and traditions depicted by the author. The film can be called the exquisite scroll of Japanese classic beauty. Not only does it include family love that builds traditional values, it also covers modern love in the new era. What is truly worth praising is the fact that the classic Japanese beauty has been constructed throughout the film.

8 Collapse of Film System and Ascendance of Independent Filmmaking

Compared with the 70s, Japan's film studios seemed to further decline in the 80s. This trend deeply affected aspects such as filmmaking, distribution and publicity. 1986 saw the rock bottom, as the three major film studios only made 24 films in total.

Under these circumstances, the old same-time scheduled release of a film in all cinemas in the country no longer worked. Neither could studios simply depend on a few major feature films to gauge the market. In the 80s, large-sized cinemas, the byproducts of industrialization of film, started to shut down one after another. Smaller-scaled cinemas that could hold about 200 people took their place. These new cinemas were no longer limited by the scheduled release of feature film system; instead, they would show films they believe would sell well, based on their own judgments. Therefore, the number of artistic films from around the world shown in Tokyo far surpassed other countries and regions. The drastic increase of these small cinemas also provided an unprecedented opportunity for new talents in the film industry.

As a result, people from all walks of life swarmed into the cinema circle. Many filmmakers would invite celebrities to participate; many musicians, writers, artists, and famous athletes also participated in making films. Some of these films were documentaries; some might even be experimental products of directors holding an 8mm video camera. Though many people tried their hands on filmmaking, very few stayed on.

In the meantime, many enterprises that had nothing to do with cinema started to invest in filmmaking; many businesses and distribution companies gained more influence on the film industry through investing in film studios or supporting independent filmmakers. As cable TV and satellite TV became more popular, TV stations participated much more frequently in filmmaking and even became one of the major filmmakers.

New directors entering the film industry at this time almost did not know what film studios were and most films on the market were mostly from independent filmmakers. Japanese cinema had entered a brand new era.

Chapter 7 Heisei Era 1989-2000 平成

1. Takeshi Kitano's International Fame 北野武

Takeshi Kitano (1947-) started as one half of the Manzai Duo *The Two Beats*. In 1983, cast by Nagisa Oshima, he played a role in "Merry Christmas, Mr. Lawrence", whose success gained him quick entry into the film industry. His1989 directorial debut "Violent Cop" (その男、凶暴につき, *Sono otoko, kyōbō ni tsuki*) amazed the world, taking away Best Film, Best Director, Best Actor and Best Newcomer titles of the Year in Japanese cinema. His directing and acting skills have been widely recognized ever since.

His later films such as "A Scene at the Sea" (あの夏、いちばん静かな海, *Ano natsu, ichiban shizukana umi*) and "Sonatine" (ソナチネ, *Sonachine*) continuously broke away from the conventions of traditional film and dialogue, creating his unique and charming "austere aesthetic". 1997 saw the film he directed and starred in: "Hana-bi" (はなび, *HANA-BI*). It revealed to us the real Takeshi and his exploration and reflections on life and himself. This film earned the Golden Lion award in the Venice Film Festival, thus garnering him international fame that was considered by some as almost equal to Akira Kurosawa's.

Takeshi Kitano's films all contain the "cold and cruel" quality; his almost never changing dull stare and expression are considered the best manifestations of his "cold violence" style. He has always appeared in his films as someone fighting against the existing system yet unable to escape from the evil system. In fact, his films, set in surreal worlds, often allude to struggles against the limitations of identity. As shown in his works, those who break rules often do not fare well in the end. This could be his way of attacking Japan's social tendency of replacing individualism with collectivism, which, to him, seemed undoubtedly pathetic. His films clearly demonstrate his nihilism, believing nothing could be trustworthy and changes are hopeless; therefore, life under his lens are filled with absurdities and slapstick humor.

After "Hana-bi", he departed from his famous crime dramas, directed and starred in "Kikujiro" (菊次郎の夏, *Kikujirō no Natsu*), a film filled with a light-hearted and moving atmosphere. "Kikujiro" steered away from his laconic characters who would burst with violence in his previous works; instead, plots and the ending were revealed in a standardized format audiences are familiar with. His usual filming crew also strived to display the freshness of summer, thus pushing its warm and loving feel to its pinnacle.

Since then, Takeshi Kitano has become more skilled and flexible and his themes have become more diverse, ranging from light comedies such as "Getting Any" (みんな〜やってるか, *Minnā yatteru ka*) to chambaras like "Zatoichi" (座頭市). His international fame has consequently been further cemented.

2. Shunji Iwai's Japanese "Pure Love" Storm 岩井俊二

Japanese cinema in the 1990s saw changes in both its themes and format. Amongst them, Shunji Iwai set off a global Japanese style "Pure Love" storm.

"Pure Love" films are mostly set in schools to narrate innocent yet heart-felt love stories in youths. They are like first loves, beautiful and oblivious, yet often end in tragedy. These "Pure Love" films undoubtedly embody Japanese people's kindness tendency; their peaceful, subtle, melancholy emotions deeply appease the potential angst and desperation in Japanese audiences, and provide them with opportunities to experience a brighter, purer, more hopeful life. In the meantime, they also create an idealized "utopia"; in a fantastical visual world devoid of any sexual or material desire, or class difference, where pure love could take place irrelevant of life or death, Japanese audiences could find their inner peace and satisfy their emotional needs. These make up the most important social basis for and psychological motivation behind the long lasting "Pure Love" films in Japan.

Shunji Iwai (1963-) is the central figure in this storm. His 1995 "Love Letter" (ラヴレター) actually launched the "Pure Love". The film first shocked Japanese audiences with its fresh and moving plots and aesthetical images; its impact then quickly reached Southeast Asia and even Europe and America. Shunji Iwai's later representative works such as "April Story" (四月物語, *Shigatsu monogatari*) and "All About Lily Chou-Chou" (リリイ・シュシュのすべて, *Riri Shushu no subete*) have also been considered classic "Pure Love" films. In 2004, he also directed his first comedy "Hana & Alice" (花とアリス, *Hanato arisu*), for which he composed the film score himself. Popular idols at the time Anne Suzuki (鈴木杏) and Yu Aoi (蒼井優) costarred in it, putting on vivid display adolescents' innocence, friendship and subtle love, and evoking another wave of strong response amongst young audiences. On the other hand, his darker films that do not fit the "Pure Love" category, such as "Swallowtail Butterfly" (スワロウテイル・バタフライ) and "Undo" (アンドゥ) were unable to produce as strong an impact.

The effect of this "Pure Love" storm started by Shunji Iwai continued to grow and expand. Not only did it set the trend for Japan, the whole world also followed suit. Places in Korea, Taiwain, even Europe and America thereupon saw the appearance of many "Pure Love" films that depicted the innocent love amongst youths, all of which had great influence on local film markets. Many youngsters have been wrapped up in these sweet and beautiful love stories that long linger in their mind.

3 Japanese Psychological Thriller Trend

While Japanese "Pure Love" storm was at its height, another cinema trend also launched in Japan was spreading rapidly, with its effect spilling out of Japan and reaching Europe and America, the psychological thriller.

Japanese psychological thrillers differ from Euro American ones that depend on special effects and blood and guts to create horror; instead, they use creepy and terrifying images and sound effects, in the meantime, exploiting the minds of audiences in order to create a horrifying atmosphere. Deeply affected by the traditions of Eastern mysticism, the horror created by these Japanese thrillers does not result from visual stimulations, but the imaginations of audiences. The ghostly images from films like "Ring" (リング, *Ringu*) and "Hanako of the Toilet" (トイレのはなこさん, *Toireno hanakosan*) are all uncertain ethereal phantoms. Their filming techniques present flashy, evanescent ghost appearances that thicken audiences' anticipations and further build up fear and horror in their minds. They embody the aesthetical focus on feelings and enjoyment, something well done in the East Asian culture, and have a strong hint of Eastern metaphysics. Meanwhile, props used in these thrillers are all daily necessities, such as tapes, phones, hair, mirrors, shadows, water, deserted buildings and some other weird oddities. The real horror does not originate from strangely shaped monsters, but an icy stare, an evil smirk, and some other mysterious taboos that you desire to know yet stay unknown and mysterious.

These psychological thrillers understand the minds of audiences and accurately pinch their sensitive nerves, bringing fresh air to Europe and America, where thrillers were bogged in blood and guts. Hollywood quickly followed this trend and remade a large quantity of these Japanese thrillers. The box office success of films like "Ring" and "Ju-on: The Grudge" (呪怨じゅおん) was soon followed by a Hollywood remake. Unfortunately, most of these remakes are considered inferior to their Japanese originals, as the rich mysterious atmosphere from the east is lost and the horror effects are thereupon greatly discounted in the remakes.

Kiyoshi Kurosawa 黒沢清

Kiyoshi Kurosawa (1955-) is one of the directors most representative of the psychological thriller genre. He is also one of the few who has truly formed his own distinctive style.

1983 saw the beginning of his directorial career with a pink film at Nikkatsu "Kandagawa Pervert Wars"(神田川淫乱戦争, *Kandagawa Inran Sensō*), but what really earned him fame are the series of thrillers he directed in the 1990s, with "Cure"(キュア, *Kyua*) being the best. Filmed in 1997, it instilled impudence and insolence into daily life, crafting elliptical and confusing atmosphere of horror; it also integrated the postmodern musings of intellectuals into the reflection of the social alienation trend.

The ensuing "License to Live" (ニンゲン合格, *Ningen gokaku*) unexpectedly explored humanistic family problems and left some rare sense of warmth in his dark cold world while traversing between realities and illusions. His 1999 "Charisma" (カリスマ, *Karisuma*) is a fable rich in symbolism, showcasing Kiyoshi Kurosawa's pessimism through a journey of doom. His 2001 "Pulse" (回路, *Kairo*) continued to explore the theme of doom and has been considered his most ambitious work. This peaceful, meticulous yet depressing horror reveals alienation amongst people while they are addicted to conveniences high tech brings; it reflects the dark and hopeless mindset, the long-drawn-out life, and the inescapable ultimate loneliness in nihilism, which Japanese nationals seemed to hold during the economic recession. The film also proposed most doomsday interpretations and refused easy explanations from audiences about the sources of horror, thus emitting an even heavier and more inescapable feel. "Pulse" has also been remade in Hollywood under the same name.

Other than "Pulse", "Barren Illusions"(いなる幻影, *Ōinaru gen'ei*) and "Séance" (降霊, *Kōrei*) series are amongst his psychological thriller oeuvre. All of them, rich in Kiyoshi Kurosawa's unique style, established his significant position in this genre.

4. A New Generation of Leaders in Anime

In the anime industry, an indispensable pillar for Japanese cinema, a new generation of leaders came into play. They have not only inherited the ideas and concepts of the older generation of anime masters, but also pushed Japanese anime to a new height with their newer techniques and themes. They undoubtedly include Satoshi Kon (今敏) and Mamoru Oshii (押井守).

Satoshi Kon 今敏

Satoshi Kon (1963-2010) was once Katsuhiro Otomo's artist in "Roujin Z", which officially started his long term cooperation with Otomo and launched him into the anime industry. He was clearly influenced by Otomo in many aspects ranging from manga's montage technique to the use of bright and heavy colors. Satoshi Kon himself once said that he was greatly affected by Katsuhiro Otomo's works like "Domu: A Child's Dream" (童夢, *Dōmu*) and "Akira".

His 1997 "Perfect Blue" (パーフェクトブルー, *Pāfekuto Burū*) was the film that truly attracted the attention of the anime world. Its seamless blending of imagination and reality seemed extremely striking and avant-garde. Since then, his style of starting from reality, mixing with imagination and ending with pure imagination has begun to mature. His 2001 masterpiece "Millennium Actress" (千年女優, *Sennen Joyū*), though only Satoshi Kon's second anime, garnered many big awards and earned critical acclaim both in and outside Japan. It depicted the dramatic life of an actress. Across time and space, audiences are taken on a supernatural journey that mixes illusion and reality and covers life both on and off the silver screen. With its unique setup, touching plots, smooth camera movement and set management, the whole story seems richer and more lifelike. Along with Hayao Miyazaki's "Spirited Away", it was considered the best animated film of the year.

The subsequent "Tokyo Godfathers" (東京ゴッドファーザーズ, *Tōkyō Goddofāzāzu*), though seemingly not matching the massive narrative framework and the history and spirit of Japanese nationals in "Millennium Actress", takes audiences back to the modern Japanese life. It uses the familiar streets and sightseeing locations in Tokyo to display a bizarre search filled with laughter and joy. The three homeless characters in the film projected the reality of modern Japan, the cruelty under economic changes and the hard life of the common people.

His later "Paranoia Agent" (妄想代理人, *Mōsō Dairinin*) and "Paprika" (パプリカ) further deployed and fine-tuned his unconstrained imagination to create a dreamy world. Those surreal and futuristic shots have also become the best embodiment of his artistic talent.

Sadly, this anime genius died prematurely in his forties. His unfinished dreams can only be there awaiting others to complete.

Mamoru Oshii 押井守

Mamoru Oshii (1951-) was brought into the spotlight since directing "Urusei Yatsura" (うる星やつら) series. It earned quite a few praises in Japan and East Asia. Apart from matching the original manga spirit, he also added a large amount of his own take in the production, which successfully conveyed unique individual thoughts and attracted wide attention from different fields. What took his career to a new height would be his 1998 "Patlabor" (機動警察パトレイバー the Movie, *Kidō keisatsu patoreibā* the movie), whose success has been universally recognized.

The film that truly gained Mamoru Oshii fame in the world of anime would be his "Ghost in the Shell" (攻殻機動隊, *Kōkaku Kidōtai*). It has been regarded as the most cutting-edge in Japanese anime. Portraying the fine line between reality and cyber world, it has far reaching effects on Euro American sci-fi films such as "The Matrix". Soon afterwards, it hit Hollywood and garnered universal high acclaim, thus making it an anime classic of Japanese anime.

Momoru Oshii has since been regarded as an equal representative of Japanese anime as Hayao Miyazaki and Katsuhiro Otomo. However, as his themes are comparatively obscure, and he has not produced any more significant films, his influence seems to be on the decline.

5. Mid-career Directors: Homage to Traditions

Amongst mid-career directors of this period, two coincided with each other in finding their inspiration in traditional Japanese films. In Yasujiro Ozu's conventional shots, they gained their revelation, carried on the legacy, and built upon those traditions. These are Masayuki Suo (周防正行) and Hirokazu Koreeda (是枝裕和).

Masayuki Suo 周防正行

Masayuki Suo (1956-) made his directorial debut "Abnormal Family: Older Brother's Bride" (変態家族兄貴の嫁さん, *Hentai kazoku: Aniki no yomesan*) in 1984. This pink film was designed as a complete tribute to Ozu, including elements such as Shochiku's company logo in the beginning, the characters' names, the 18 degree low angle upward static shots, and the layout of the sets. Masayuki Suo carefully and ingeniously, almost entirely, modeled after Ozu's filming techniques in this production. A famous Japanese film scholar Shigehiko Hasumi once said, "'Abnormal Family' has been so influenced by Yasujiro Ozu that it could almost be regarded as the showcase of Ozu's styles from different periods."

However, the copying of Ozu's techniques is not superficial; it actually shows Masayuki Suo's true admiration towards his predecessors. What he really tried to model after was the appeal of Ozu's films to both refined and popular taste. His later works indicated he was able to achieve that goal.

His 1989 "Fancy Dance" (ファンシィダンス) and 1992 "Sumo Do, Sumo Don't" (シコふんじゃった, *Shiko funjatta*) seemed quite parallel and belonged to youth comedy genre. Both are touching and inspiring, leaving smiling audiences in the end. The films aimed to encourage people to support each other and advance bravely, as in their traditions.

His 1996 "Shall We Dance?" (Shall we ダンス?, *Sharu wi Dansu*) depicted a successful man taking up ballroom dancing classes while going through his mid-life crisis. Through his dance lessons, he met different characters who have found motivation and courage for life through dancing. This film is meticulous yet full of tender feelings, subtle yet humorous. The troublesome and frustrating mid-life crisis has then been resolved in the warmest and most graceful way. Tamiyo Kusakari, whom Masayuki Suo later married, also put on an amazing performance. After its release, not only did it do well in box office, it also earned critical acclaim, showing his success in handling commercial films.

Eleven years later, he made a comeback with his 2007 "Even So, I Didn't Do It." (そ
れでもボクはやってない, *Soredemo boku wa yattenai*) It was based on a true story and
had a tinge of dark humor, solemnly exploring the justice system and criticizing
malpractice in the existing system. The film was a financial hit, yielding over 1 billion yen
in box office. It also won Best Film of the Year according to Kinema Junpo.

Masayuki Suo is not a prolific director; however, all of his films have maintained a
high standard. Furthermore, his works have achieved a difficult balance between
commercial and artistic values. They are able to draw and keep audiences while
reaching for high artistic grounds. Masayuki Suo has also been considered as one of the
strongest directors in Japan.

Hirokazu Koreeda 是枝裕和

It has been said that if Masayuki Suo paid his tribute to Ozu with modeling after
Ozu's filming techniques, Hirokazu Koreeda (1962-) could be said as the one continuing
on Ozu's themes: family and humanities.

Hirokazu Koreeda is an outstanding representative of the new generation of 90s'
directors in Japan's independent film industry. His works mostly show concern over the
society and are humanistic.

His 1995 "Trick of the Light" (幻の光, *Maboroshi no Hikari*) was his first feature film.
Its release immediately caught wide attention from all fields, later winning many awards
both in and outside Japan. The film explored themes of love and loss, hope and rebirth.
Through unfolding the story of a woman losing family members several times, it put on

display "life and death" and "loss and rebirth".

His subsequent "After Life" (ワンダフルライフ, *Wandafuru Raifu*) broke free from the mainstream films that dealt with death and projected a ghost story filled with human warmth. His later "Distance"(ディスタンス) and "Nobody Knows" (誰も知らない, *Dare mo Shiranai*) were both well received for the guileless emotions depicted. The leading roles are an ordinary family, just like the real families like and around us.

His 2008 "Still Walking" (歩いても 歩いても, *Aruitemo aruitemo*) is said to have epitomized the essence of Ozu's works. Its plots and themes are plain and simple, not garish. It does not have societal problems to attract audiences, nor does it contain thrilling or novel content. The leading roles are an ordinary family - Yokoyamas, just like the ones in reality. This family has quite a tricky structure that can really be broken down into three types of sub-families. Hirokazu Koreeda only depicted 24 hours of Yokoyamas' life, everything that took place over the course of one day. Daily dialogues amongst the characters pushed the plots along, revealing intricate relationships in the family's over decades of history. The title itself "Still Walking" concealed the characters' state of mind – Even though they have been walking, they seemed to have always taken just one step too late. In the meantime, the film also mirrored the director's reflections on life as Hirokazau Koreeda lost both of his parents around that time. It did not try to preach any human law or principle; instead; the director focused on life in its truest form and sought to capture the inner worlds of common people.

Hirokazu Koreeda's films are always simple and plain without dramatic plots and themes or glaring filming techniques. His lens is always pointed at ordinary families' ordinary lives, aiming to portray the authentic life. This authenticity is exactly why his films can strike a responsive chord in his audiences.

6. Other Important Directors

In the 1990s, Japanese film industry blossomed. A great variety of directors stepped into the spotlight through independent or experimental filmmaking. Myriads of them have made great contributions to the rejuvenation of Japanese cinema through their stylized works. A few of the important directors are briefly introduced below.

Yoshimitsu Morita 森田芳光

Yoshimitsu Morita (森田芳光) (1950-2011) earned instant fame with his 1981 "Something Like It" (の・ようなもの, *No Yōna Mono*), promoting himself from making 8mm shorts to making 35mm feature films, skipping a total of 16mm. What stood out are its filming techniques and its portrayal of modern youth. It earned wide acclaim with its unique humor and satire.

His 1983 "The Family Game" (家族ゲーム, *Kazoku gēmu*) is based on Yohei Honma's novel. It described the story that took place in a strict family, amongst parents, their sons (secondary school students), and their private tutor who advocated use of violence. Morita's sharp observation and insight into characters and his genius picture composition (the original dinner scene where everyone ate in one row) made the film a representative work of outstanding family dramas in 80s' Japanese cinema. Using black humor, he incisively criticized the way modern Japanese families live their life and educate their children. It pocketed all film awards of the year in Japan and ranked number one in Kinema Junpo's Top Ten list.

In 1985, he filmed "Sorekara" (それから, lit. "And Then"), deeply portraying the conflicted inner world of a reticent man who fell in love with his friend's wife. It was adapted from a work of the famous writer Natsume Soseki (夏目漱石). Morita used modern methods to reinterpret the story from the Meiji period, presenting the classy style of Japanese literary and artistic films. It revealed his original artistic foundation and swept many awards.

Once into the 1990s, Yoshimitsu Morita acutely sensed new trends and created works such as "Future Memories: Last Christmas" (未来の想い出, *Mirai no omoide*) (1992), "Haru" (1996), "A Lost Paradise" (失楽園, *Shitsurakuen*) (1997) to portray the sentiments in the internet age and post Japanese economic collapse period. All of these films left deep impressions on audiences. "A Lost Paradise" pushed his career to a new height. It depicted a painful extramarital affair between a middle-aged couple, which shocked the whole country and was a social phenomenon that was widely discussed after the film release. In fact, his films of this period are mostly of high social value and their themes often stimulate heated conversations amongst audiences.

Sion Sono 園子温

Sion Sono (1962-) started writing modern poems at the age of 17 to ridicule the dark society and the human nature. They were well received by young readers and he was considered a genius poet. After he dropped out of university, he started working in filmmaking and his films still mainly focus on exploring human nature and social system.

His 2005 "Noriko's Dinner Table" (紀子の食卓, *Noriko no shokutaku*) was his first film that caught people's attention. It vividly depicted family relationships and sentiments behind the coming of age. The slightly perverted "family rental" social support behavior cast light upon many ordinary Japanese people's state of mind: loneliness, desperation, schizophrenia, with death being the end of everything. The scene of 54 girls' group suicide – jumping in front of a train hand in hand – remains disturbing, shocking and chilling.

His subsequent "Strange Circus" (奇妙なサーカス, *Kimyô na sâkasu*) used exaggerated sets, such as a blood-covered hallway in the school, and an array of aggrandized masks in the circus. All of these showed a ceremonial sense the director had bestowed upon the film, permeating it with perverted extreme insanity that resulted from desperation. The lust of the characters became confused due to conflicts with reality; their desire to redeem oneself led to deeper desperation. The film adopted the multi-layered narrative technique, with characters shuttling back and forth, creating a confusing illusion between reality and fiction.

Sion Sono's other representative works such as "Love Exposure" (愛のむきだし, *Ai no mukidashi*) (2008), "Cold Fish" (冷たい熱帯魚, *Tsumetai nettaigyo*) (2010) and "Guilty of Romance" (恋の罪, *Koi no tsumi*) (2011) continued in the same style. His films are filled with elements such as morbidity, distortion, filth, sex, extremeness, and violence. However, behind those, we can still see exquisite, deeply-felt, gentle, sweet and sad sentiments. Exactly through his realistic, poetic, cruel aesthetics, Sion Sono is able to make his own mark in Japanese film industry.

Epilogue

Japanese film history spans over more than 100 years and this book's few words certainly fail to cover all of its rich and wonderful content. A large number of key characters and events have only been briefly mentioned or even been omitted, which is an unavoidable regret. Through succinct recounts and introductions, the book aims to open the door for those who love Japanese films and culture. The true wonders of the Japanese film world await readers behind that door.

www.ingramcontent.com/pod-product-compliance
Lightning Source LLC
Chambersburg PA
CBHW071241170526
45165CB00003B/1194